SOLUTIONS MANUAL
AND STUDY GUIDE

Fundamentals of Futures and Options Markets

Seventh Edition

Skip 8-5
9-5 and 9-20
10-17 to 10-21

John C. Hull

Maple Financial Group Professor of
Derivatives and Risk Management
Joseph L. Rotman School of Management
University of Toronto

Pearson Prentice Hall, Upper Saddle River, NJ 07458

Acquisitions Editor: Tessa O'Brien
Editorial Assistant: Kerri McQueen
Production Editor: Alison Eusden
Manufacturing Buyer: Linda Cox

Copyright© 2011, 2008, 2005, 2002, 1998 Pearson Education, Inc., 75 Arlington Street, Boston, MA 02116. Pearson Prentice Hall. All rights reserved. Printed in the United States of America. This publication is protected by copyright and permission should be obtained from the publisher prior to any prohibited reproduction, storage in a retrieval system, or transmission in any form or by any means, electronic, mechanical, photocopying, recording, or likewise. For information regarding permission(s), write to: Rights and Permissions Department.

This work is protected by United States copyright laws and is provided solely for the use of instructors in teaching their courses and assessing student learning. Dissemination or sale of any part of this work (including on the World Wide Web) will destroy the integrity of the work and is not permitted. The work and materials from it should never be made available to students except by instructors using the accompanying text in their classes. All recipients of this work are expected to abide by these restrictions and to honor the intended pedagogical purposes and the needs of other instructors who rely on these materials.

Pearson Prentice Hall™ is a trademark of Pearson Education, Inc.

Prentice Hall
is an imprint of

www.pearsonhighered.com

1 2 3 4 5 6 BB 13 12 11 10

ISBN-13: 978-0-13-610291-5
ISBN-10: 0-13-610291-3

Contents

Preface

This book contains solutions to the questions and problems that appear at the ends of chapters in my book *Fundamentals of Futures and Options Markets*, 7th edition. The questions and problems have been designed to help readers study on their own and test their understanding of the material. They range from quick checks on whether a key point is understood to much more challenging applications of analytical techniques. To maximize the benefits from this book readers are urged to sketch out their own solutions to the problems before consulting mine.

At the beginning of each chapter I have included a summary of the main points in the chapter and suggested ways readers should approach studying the material in the chapter. You should find this material useful both when you first cover the material in the chapter and when you are studying for exams.

I welcome comments on either *Fundamentals of Futures and Options Markets*, 7th edition or this book. My e-mail address is

hull@rotman.utoronto.ca

John C. Hull
Joseph L. Rotman School of Management
University of Toronto

CHAPTER 1
Introduction

This chapter introduces futures, forward, and option contracts and explains the types of traders that use them. If you already know how futures, forward, and options work you will not have to spend too much time on this chapter. Note that Chapter 1 does not distinguish between futures and forward contracts. Both are agreements to buy or sell an asset at a certain time in the future for a certain price. It is Chapter 2 that covers the daily settlement feature of futures contracts and itemizes the differences between the two sorts of contracts.

Make sure you understand the key difference between futures (or forwards) and options. Futures and forward contracts are obligations to enter into a transaction in the future. An option is the right to enter into a transaction in the future. A futures or forward contract may prove to be an asset or a liability (depending on the future price of the underlying asset). An option contract is a always an asset to the buyer of the option and a liability to the seller of the contract. It costs money (the option premium) to purchase an option. Normally no money (except margin requirements which are discussed in Chapter 2) change hands when a futures or forward contract is entered into. Table 1.1 shows forward foreign exchange quotes. Table 1.2 show the prices of options on Google. Make sure you understand what the numbers in these tables mean and how the profit diagrams in Figure 1.3 are constructed.

The distinction between over-the-counter and exchange-traded markets is important. Exchange-traded markets are markets where the contracts are defined by an exchange such as the Chicago Board of Trade. How trading is done, how payments flow from one side to the other, and so on is determined by the exchange. The over-the-counter (OTC) market is primarily a market between financial institutions, non-financial corporations, and fund managers. They typically communicate and agree on trades by phone or electronically. An exchange is not involved. However, as a result of regulatory initiatives many OTC trades are expected to move to clearinghouses and exchanges. As Figure 1.2 indicates, the OTC market was about ten times the size of the exchange-traded market at the end of 2008. The open-outcry system in exchanges is an arrangement where traders meet on the floor of the exchange and use hand signals to indicate the trades they would like to do. This is increasingly being replaced by electronic trading where traders sit at terminals and use a keyboard to indicate the trades they would like to do.

The chapter identifies the three main types of traders that uses forward, futures, and options markets. *Hedgers* use the markets to reduce their risk exposure to a market variable such as an exchange rate, a commodity price, or an interest rate. *Speculators* use the market to take a position on the future direction of a market variable. *Arbitrageurs* attempt to lock in a riskless profit by simultaneously entering into transactions in two or more markets. The chapter gives examples of the activities of the three types of traders. Hedge funds (see Business Snapshot 1.1) use derivatives for all three purposes. As the

SocGen example (Business Snapshot 1.2) shows, one of the dangers in derivatives markets is that a trader will use derivatives for unauthorized speculation and lose a lot of money before superiors find out what is going on.

SOLUTIONS TO PRACTICE QUESTIONS

Problem 1.8.

Suppose you own 5,000 shares that are worth $25 each. How can put options be used to provide you with insurance against a decline in the value of your holding over the next four months?

You should buy 50 put option contracts (each on 100 shares) with a strike price of $25 and an expiration date in four months. If at the end of four months the stock price proves to be less than $25, you can exercise the options and sell the shares for $25 each.

Problem 1.9.

A stock when it is first issued provides funds for a company. Is the same true of an exchange-traded stock option? Discuss.

An exchange-traded stock option provides no funds for the company. It is a security sold by one investor to another. The company is not involved. By contrast, a stock when it is first issued is sold by the company to investors and does provide funds for the company.

Problem 1.10.

Explain why a futures contract can be used for either speculation or hedging.

If an investor has an exposure to the price of an asset, he or she can hedge with futures contracts. If the investor will gain when the price decreases and lose when the price increases, a long futures position will hedge the risk. If the investor will lose when the price decreases and gain when the price increases, a short futures position will hedge the risk. Thus either a long or a short futures position can be entered into for hedging purposes.

If the investor has no exposure to the price of the underlying asset, entering into a futures contract is speculation. If the investor takes a long position, he or she gains when the asset's price increases and loses when it decreases. If the investor takes a short position, he or she loses when the asset's price increases and gains when it decreases.

Problem 1.11.

A cattle farmer expects to have 120,000 pounds of live cattle to sell in three months. The live-cattle futures contract on the Chicago Mercantile Exchange is for the delivery of 40,000 pounds of cattle. How can the farmer use the contract for hedging? From the farmer's viewpoint, what are the pros and cons of hedging?

The farmer can short 3 contracts that have 3 months to maturity. If the price of cattle falls, the gain on the futures contract will offset the loss on the sale of the cattle. If the price of cattle rises, the gain on the sale of the cattle will be offset by the loss on the futures contract. Using futures contracts to hedge has the advantage that it can at no

2

cost reduce risk to almost zero. Its disadvantage is that the farmer no longer gains from favorable movements in cattle prices.

Problem 1.12.

It is July 2010. A mining company has just discovered a small deposit of gold. It will take six months to construct the mine. The gold will then be extracted on a more or less continuous basis for one year. Futures contracts on gold are available on the New York Mercantile Exchange. There are delivery months every two months from August 2010 to December 2011. Each contract is for the delivery of 100 ounces. Discuss how the mining company might use futures markets for hedging.

The mining company can estimate its production on a month by month basis. It can then short futures contracts to lock in the price received for the gold. For example, if a total of 3,000 ounces are expected to be produced in September 2010 and October 2010, the price received for this production can be hedged by shorting a total of 30 October 2010 contracts.

Problem 1.13.

Suppose that a March call option on a stock with a strike price of $50 costs $2.50 and is held until March. Under what circumstances will the holder of the option make a gain? Under what circumstances will the option be exercised? Draw a diagram showing how the profit on a long position in the option depends on the stock price at the maturity of the option.

The holder of the option will gain if the price of the stock is above $52.50 in March. (This ignores the time value of money.) The option will be exercised if the price of the stock is above $50.00 in March. The profit as a function of the stock price is shown in Figure S1.1.

Figure S1.1   Profit from long position in Problem 1.13

3

Problem 1.14.

Suppose that a June put option on a stock with a strike price of $60 costs $4 and is held until June. Under what circumstances will the holder of the option make a gain? Under what circumstances will the option be exercised? Draw a diagram showing how the profit on a short position in the option depends on the stock price at the maturity of the option.

The seller of the option will lose if the price of the stock is below $56.00 in June. (This ignores the time value of money.) The option will be exercised if the price of the stock is below $60.00 in June. The profit as a function of the stock price is shown in Figure S1.2.

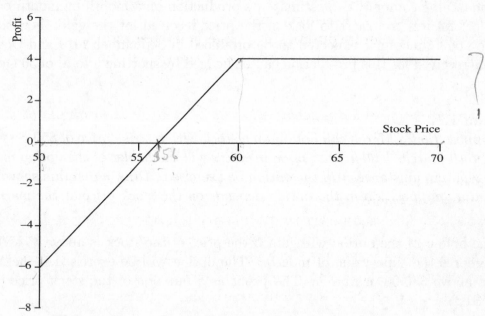

Figure S1.2   Profit from short position In Problem 1.14

Problem 1.15.

It is May and a trader writes a September call option with a strike price of $20. The stock price is $18, and the option price is $2. Describe the investor's cash flows if the option is held until September and the stock price is $25 at this time.

The trader has an inflow of $2 in May and an outflow of $5 in September. The $2 is the cash received from the sale of the option. The $5 is the result of the option being exercised. The investor has to buy the stock for $25 in September and sell it to the purchaser of the option for $20.

Problem 1.16.

An investor writes a December put option with a strike price of $30. The price of the option is $4. Under what circumstances does the investor make a gain?

The investor makes a gain if the price of the stock is above $26 at the time of exercise. (This ignores the time value of money.) *below* $30-4=26

Problem 1.17.

The Chicago Board of Trade offers a futures contract on long-term Treasury bonds. Characterize the investors likely to use this contract.

Most investors will use the contract because they want to do one of the following:
(a) Hedge an exposure to long-term interest rates. ✓
(b) Speculate on the future direction of long-term interest rates. ✓
(c) Arbitrage between the spot and futures markets for Treasury bonds. ✓

Problem 1.18.

An airline executive has argued: "There is no point in our using oil futures. There is just as much chance that the price of oil in the future will be less than the futures price as there is that it will be greater than this price." Discuss the executive's viewpoint.

It may well be true that there is just as much chance that the price of oil in the future will be above the futures price as that it will be below the futures price. This means that the use of a futures contract for speculation would be like betting on whether a coin comes up heads or tails. But it might make sense for the airline to use futures for hedging rather than speculation. The futures contract then has the effect of reducing risks. It can be argued that an airline should not expose its shareholders to risks associated with the future price of oil when there are contracts available to hedge the risks.

Problem 1.19.

"Options and futures are zero-sum games." What do you think is meant by this statement?

The statement means that the gain (loss) to the party with the short position is equal to the loss (gain) to the party with the long position. In total, the gain to all parties is zero.

Problem 1.20.

A trader enters into a short forward contract on 100 million yen. The forward exchange rate is $0.0080 per yen. How much does the trader gain or lose if the exchange rate at the end of the contract is (a) $0.0074 per yen; (b) $0.0091 per yen?

(a) The trader sells 100 million yen for $0.0080 per yen when the exchange rate is $0.0074 per yen. The gain is 100×0.0006 millions of dollars or $60,000.
(b) The trader sells 100 million yen for $0.0080 per yen when the exchange rate is $0.0091 per yen. The loss is 100×0.0011 millions of dollars or $110,000.

Problem 1.21.

A trader enters into a short cotton futures contract when the futures price is 50 cents per pound. The contract is for the delivery of 50,000 pounds. How much does the trader gain or lose if the cotton price at the end of the contract is (a) 48.20 cents per pound; (b) 51.30 cents per pound?

(a) The trader sells for 50 cents per pound something that is worth 48.20 cents per pound. Gain $= (\$0.5000 - \$0.4820) \times 50,000 = \$900$.

(b) The trader sells for 50 cents per pound something that is worth 51.30 cents per pound. Loss $= (\$0.5130 - \$0.5000) \times 50,000 = \$650$.

Problem 1.22.

A company knows that it is due to receive a certain amount of a foreign currency in four months. What type of option contract is appropriate for hedging?

A long position in a four-month put option can provide insurance against the exchange rate falling below the strike price. It ensures that the foreign currency can be sold for at least the strike price.

Problem 1.23.

A United States company expects to have to pay 1 million Canadian dollars in six months. Explain how the exchange rate risk can be hedged using (a) a forward contract; (b) an option.

The company could enter into a long forward contract to buy 1 million Canadian dollars in six months. This would have the effect of locking in an exchange rate equal to the current forward exchange rate. Alternatively the company could buy a call option giving it the right (but not the obligation) to purchase 1 million Canadian dollar at a certain exchange rate in six months. This would provide insurance against a strong Canadian dollar in six months while still allowing the company to benefit from a weak Canadian dollar at that time.

6

CHAPTER 2
Mechanics of Futures Markets

This chapter covers the details of how futures markets work. Three key things you should understand are a) how futures contracts are entered into and closed out, b) how the daily settlement procedures work, and c) the operation of margin accounts.

A long futures contract is an agreement to buy a certain amount of the underlying asset during a future month; a short futures contract is an agreement to sell a certain amount of the underlying asset during a future month. You can enter into a futures contract (long or short) by issuing appropriate instructions to your broker. Let's use the hogs-lean futures contracts in Table 2.2 as an example. Each contract is on 40,000 pounds of hogs. Suppose you short (i.e., sell) one October contract on August 4, 2009. (The High and Low columns in Table 2.2 indicate that the futures price at the time of your transaction is between 49.325 and 52.575 cents per pound.) Your broker will ask you to prove that you are capable of honoring your commitments by making a deposit. This deposit is known as the initial margin and minimum initial margin levels per contract are specified by the exchange. The broker uses the initial margin deposit to open a margin account for you.

The settlement price on the contract (fifth column in Table 2.2) determines the daily settlement process (known as marking to market the contract). The settlement price for a day is the price at which the contract trades at the close of trading on that day. It is 50.125 for the contract we are considering on August 4, 2009. If the settlement price on April hogs increases by 2 cents per pound from one day to the next you lose $0.02 \times 40,000 = \$800$ from your margin account. (Because you have a short position, futures price increases cost you money). Similarly, if the settlement price on April hogs decreases by 2 cents per pound from one day to the next $800 would be added to your margin account. A maintenance margin (usually about 75% of the initial margin) is specified. If the balance in the margin account falls below the maintenance margin level you get a margin call from your broker requiring you to bring the balance in your margin account up to the initial margin level. If you do not provide the necessary funds within 24 hours your position is closed out. Study the gold futures example in Table 2.1 and make sure you understand all the entries in the table.

When you instruct your broker to close out your futures position (or when the broker closes you out because you fail to meet a margin call) the broker does the opposite trade to the original one on your behalf. For example, suppose you decided you wanted to close out your short-one-contract April hogs futures position on September 5, 2009. Your broker would contact the exchange to enter into a long April hogs contract on your behalf. The long contract would cancel out the short contract and you would be left with no outstanding position. One of the attractions of futures contracts is that it is just as easy to take a long as a short position. Another is that it is just as easy to close out a position as to enter into it in the first place.

Most futures contracts are closed out prior to the delivery period, but some do lead to delivery. It is the possibility of final delivery that ties the futures price to the spot price. When delivery takes place it is the party with the short futures position that initiates delivery. The party with the short position may have some choices to make on exactly what is delivered, where it is delivered, and when it is delivered. Some contracts such as futures on stock indices are settled in cash rather than by physical delivery. In these cases a single delivery date is specified for the contract. The contract is marked to market until this delivery date. On the delivery date there is a final daily settlement, based on the spot value of the underlying asset, and all contracts are declared closed out.

One of the attractions of futures contracts for speculators is that they have built in leverage. The amount of cash you have to provide to do a trade (the initial margin) is a relatively small percentage of the value of asset being traded (perhaps only 10%).

When you trade stocks there are many different types of orders that can be placed with a broker: market orders, limit orders, stop orders, stop-loss orders, and so on. As Section 2.8 indicates, the same types of orders can be placed in futures markets. The accounting and tax treatment of futures and other derivatives is complicated, but Section 2.10 provides an overview of the issues that are important in many jurisdictions. Normal accrual accounting leads to the profit or loss on a futures transaction being recognized throughout the life of the contract for both accounting and tax purposes. However, if a trader can show that a contract is entered into for hedging purposes, then the profit or loss on the contract is recognized when the contract is closed out. (See Example 2.1.) The idea here is that for a hedger the cash flows from the futures contract should be matched with the cash flows from the underlying asset being hedged.

You should by now be fully comfortable with the differences between futures and forward contracts. These are summarized in Table 2.3. Both futures and forwards are agreements to buy or sell an asset at a future time for a future price. Futures contracts are traded on an exchange; forward contracts are traded over-the counter. Futures contracts have standard terms defined by the exchange for the size of the contract, delivery dates, etc; forward contracts are not standardized. Delivery in a futures contract can often take place on a number of different days during the delivery month; forward contracts normally have only one delivery date specified. Futures contracts are settled daily by the transfer of funds into or out of the margin account; forward contracts are settled at the end of the contract. Futures contracts are normally closed out prior to delivery; forward contracts are normally held to delivery. The margins and daily settlement in futures contracts have the effect of eliminating virtually all credit risk; there is some (small) credit risk in forward contracts.

SOLUTIONS TO PRACTICE QUESTIONS

Problem 2.8.

The party with a short position in a futures contract sometimes has options as to the precise asset that will be delivered, where delivery will take place, when delivery will take place, and so on. Do these options increase or decrease the futures price? Explain your reasoning.

These options make the contract less attractive to the party with the long position

8

and more attractive to the party with the short position. They therefore tend to reduce the futures price.

Problem 2.9.

What are the most important aspects of the design of a new futures contract?

The most important aspects of the design of a new futures contract are the specification of the underlying asset, the size of the contract, the delivery arrangements, and the delivery months.

Problem 2.10.

Explain how margins protect investors against the possibility of default.

A margin is a sum of money deposited by an investor with his or her broker. It acts as a guarantee that the investor can cover any losses on the futures contract. The balance in the margin account is adjusted daily to reflect gains and losses on the futures contract. If losses are above a certain level, the investor is required to deposit a further margin. This system makes it unlikely that the investor will default. A similar system of margins makes it unlikely that the investor's broker will default on the contract it has with the clearinghouse member and unlikely that the clearinghouse member will default with the clearinghouse.

Problem 2.11.

A trader buys two July futures contracts on frozen orange juice. Each contract is for the delivery of 15,000 pounds. The current futures price is 160 cents per pound, the initial margin is $6,000 per contract, and the maintenance margin is $4,500 per contract. What price change would lead to a margin call? Under what circumstances could $2,000 be withdrawn from the margin account? $6000 - 4500 = 1500$
                                                                                     initial   Maintenance

There is a margin call if more than $1,500 is lost on one contract. This happens if the futures price of frozen orange juice falls by more than 10 cents to below 150 cents per lb. $2,000 can be withdrawn from the margin account if there is a gain on one contract of $1,000. This will happen if the futures price rises by 6.67 cents to 166.67 cents per lb.

Problem 2.12.

Show that, if the futures price of a commodity is greater than the spot price during the delivery period, then there is an arbitrage opportunity. Does an arbitrage opportunity exist if the futures price is less than the spot price? Explain your answer.

If the futures price is greater than the spot price during the delivery period, an arbitrageur buys the asset, shorts a futures contract, and makes delivery for an immediate profit. If the futures price is less than the spot price during the delivery period, there is no similar perfect arbitrage strategy. An arbitrageur can take a long futures position but cannot force immediate delivery of the asset. The decision on when delivery will be made is made by the party with the short position. Nevertheless companies interested in acquiring the asset will find it attractive to enter into a long futures contract and wait for delivery to be made.

Future Price is > spot price
So buy in the spot Mkt & sell in futures Mkt.

Problem 2.13.

   Explain the difference between a market-if-touched order and a stop order.

   A market-if-touched order is executed at the best available price after a trade occurs at a specified price or at a price more favorable than the specified price. A stop order is executed at the best available price after there is a bid or offer at the specified price or at a price less favorable than the specified price.

Problem 2.14.

   Explain what a stop-limit order to sell at 20.30 with a limit of 20.10 means.

   A stop-limit order to sell at 20.30 with a limit of 20.10 means that as soon as there is a bid at 20.30 the contract should be sold providing this can be done at 20.10 or a higher price. *Cannot sell for less than 20.10*

Problem 2.15.

   At the end of one day a clearinghouse member is long 100 contracts, and the settlement price is $50,000 per contract. The original margin is $2,000 per contract. On the following day the member becomes responsible for clearing an additional 20 long contracts, entered into at a price of $51,000 per contract. The settlement price at the end of this day is $50,200. How much does the member have to add to its margin account with the exchange clearinghouse?

   initial Margin on New contract

   The clearinghouse member is required to provide $20 \times \$2,000 = \$40,000$ as initial margin for the new contracts. There is a gain of $(50,200 - 50,000) \times 100 = \$20,000$ on the existing contracts. There is also a loss of $(51,000 - 50,200) \times 20 = \$16,000$ on the new contracts. The member must therefore add

initial *settlement* *Margin*
100 Contracts *$50,000 per cont.* *$2000 per contract*
Next Day *20 Contracts* *$51,000 per cont. entered*
$50,200 settlement

$$40,000 - 20,000 + 16,000 = \$36,000$$

initial *Gain* *Pay for*
Margin on *on existing* *Loss on*
New contract *contract* *New Contracts*

to the margin account.

Problem 2.16.

   On July 1, 2010, a Japanese company enters into a forward contract to buy $1 million with yen on January 1, 2011. On September 1, 2010, it enters into a forward contract to sell $1 million on January 1, 2011. Describe the profit or loss the company will make in dollars as a function of the forward exchange rates on July 1, 2010 and September 1, 2010.

   Suppose F_1 and F_2 are the forward exchange rates for the contracts entered into July 1, 2010 and September 1, 2010, and S is the spot rate on January 1, 2011. (All exchange rates are measured as yen per dollar). The payoff from the first contract is $(S - F_1)$ million yen and the payoff from the second contract is $(F_2 - S)$ million yen. The total payoff is therefore $(S - F_1) + (F_2 - S) = (F_2 - F_1)$ million yen.

Problem 2.17.

The forward price on the Swiss franc for delivery in 45 days is quoted as 1.1000. The futures price for a contract that will be delivered in 45 days is 0.9000. Explain these two quotes. Which is more favorable for an investor wanting to sell Swiss francs?

The 1.1000 forward quote is the number of Swiss francs per dollar. The 0.9000 futures quote is the number of dollars per Swiss franc. When quoted in the same way as the futures price the forward price is $1/1.1000 = 0.9091$. The Swiss franc is therefore more valuable in the forward market than in the futures market. The forward market is therefore more attractive for an investor wanting to sell Swiss francs.

Problem 2.18.

Suppose you call your broker and issue instructions to sell one July hogs contract. Describe what happens.

Hog futures are traded on the Chicago Mercantile Exchange. (See Table 2.2). The broker will request some initial margin. The order will be relayed by telephone to your broker's trading desk on the floor of the exchange (or to the trading desk of another broker).

It will be sent by messenger to a commission broker who will execute the trade according to your instructions. Confirmation of the trade eventually reaches you. If there are adverse movements in the futures price your broker may contact you to request additional margin.

Problem 2.19.

"Speculation in futures markets is pure gambling. It is not in the public interest to allow speculators to trade on a futures exchange." Discuss this viewpoint.

Speculators are important market participants because they add liquidity to the market. However, contracts must be useful for hedging as well as speculation. This is because regulators generally only approve contracts when they are likely to be of interest to hedgers as well as speculators.

Problem 2.20.

Identify the three commodities whose futures contracts in Table 2.2 have the highest open interest.

Based on the contract months listed, the answer is crude oil, corn, and sugar (world).

Problem 2.21.

What do you think would happen if an exchange started trading a contract in which the quality of the underlying asset was incompletely specified?

The contract would not be a success. Parties with short positions would hold their contracts until delivery and then deliver the cheapest form of the asset. This might well be viewed by the party with the long position as garbage! Once news of the quality problem became widely known no one would be prepared to buy the contract. This shows that futures contracts are feasible only when there are rigorous standards within an industry

11

for defining the quality of the asset. Many futures contracts have in practice failed because of the problem of defining quality.

Problem 2.22.

"When a futures contract is traded on the floor of the exchange, it may be the case that the open interest increases by one, stays the same, or decreases by one." Explain this statement.

If both sides of the transaction are entering into a new contract, the open interest increases by one. If both sides of the transaction are closing out existing positions, the open interest decreases by one. If one party is entering into a new contract while the other party is closing out an existing position, the open interest stays the same.

Problem 2.23.

Suppose that on October 24, 2010, you take a short position in an April 2011 live-cattle futures contract. You close out your position on January 21, 2011. The futures price (per pound) is 91.20 cents when you enter into the contract, 88.30 cents when you close out your position, and 88.80 cents at the end of December 2010. One contract is for the delivery of 40,000 pounds of cattle. What is your total profit? How is it taxed if you are (a) a hedger and (b) a speculator? Assume that you have a December 31 year end.

The total profit is

$$40,000 \times (0.9120 - 0.8830) = \$1,160$$

If you are a hedger this is all taxed in 2011. If you are a speculator

$$40,000 \times (0.9120 - 0.8880) = \$960$$

is taxed in 2010 and

$$40,000 \times (0.8880 - 0.8830) = \$200$$

is taxed in 2011.

CHAPTER 3
Hedging Strategies Using Futures

This chapter discusses how futures contracts can be used for hedging. If a company knows it will buy a certain asset at a certain future time, it can hedge its risk with a long futures position. The futures position is chosen so that a) if the asset price increases, the gain on the futures position offsets the extra price that has to be paid for the asset and b) if the asset price decreases the loss on the futures position is offset by the gain resulting from the lower price paid for the asset. Similarly, if a company knows it will sell a certain asset on a certain future date, it can hedge its risk with a short futures position. In this case the futures position is chosen so that a) if the asset price decreases the gain on the futures position offsets the loss on the amount realized for the asset and b) if the asset price increases, the loss on the futures position is offset by the gain resulting from the higher price realized for the asset.

If you need to review statistical concepts such as standard deviation, correlation, and linear regression you should study the first three sections of the appendix to before reading Section 3.4. If you are unfamiliar with the capital asset pricing model, you should study the last section of the appendix before reading Section 3.5.

Hedging is designed to reduce risk. As such it should be attractive to corporations. The chapter discusses three reasons why corporations in practice often do not hedge. These reasons are

1. In some instances shareholders prefer companies not to hedge a risk. This might be because the shareholders want exposure to the risk. (For example, many shareholders buy the stock of particular gold mining companies because they want an exposure to the price of gold. They do not want those companies to hedge their gold price risk. See Business Snapshot 3.1.) It may also because shareholders can diversify away the risk within their own portfolios.

2. Sometimes a company may appear to have exposure to a particular market variable when a "big picture" view of its risks indicates little or no exposure. (See for example the gold jewelry manufacturer example in Table 3.1 or the farmer in Problem 3.17.)

3. Corporate treasurers are liable to be criticized if money is lost on the futures position and gained on the underlying position being hedged—even though this was part of the risk reduction strategy. The imaginary dialogue between a treasurer and a president at the end of Section 3.2 illustrates the problem. Note that we expect to lose money on about half of the futures contracts we enter into. The purpose of the futures contracts is to reduce risk not to increase expected profits.

An important concept is basis risk. This arises because a futures contract that is held for hedging purposes is almost always closed out prior to the delivery date. (As described in the chapter the futures contract chosen normally has a delivery month later than the month when the underlying asset will be bought or sold.) The futures price on the close-out date does not equal the spot price. The basis is the spot price minus the futures price at this time. If you enter into a futures contract at time t_1 to hedge the purchase of an asset at time t_2, the price you effectively pay for the asset is the price at time t_2 adjusted for the gain/loss on the futures contract. This is the same as the futures price of the contract at time t_1 plus the basis at time t_2. Similarly, if you enter into a futures contract at time t_1 to hedge the sale of an asset at time t_2, the effective price you receive is the futures price at time t_1 plus the basis at time t_2. Examples illustrating this are Example 3.3 and Example 3.4. The futures price at time t_1 is known for certain when you initiate the hedge at time t_1. However, the basis at time t_2 is not known. The uncertainty associated with the price you pay or receive is therefore the uncertainty associated with the basis. Hence the term basis risk.

The hedge ratio is the ratio of the size of the futures position to the size of the exposure being hedged. The normal situation is to use a hedge ratio of 1.0. The chapter describes two situations where a hedge ratio of 1.0 is not appropriate. One is when there is cross hedging; the other is when stock index futures are used. Cross hedging is not hedging done in anger! It involves a situation where the asset underlying the futures contract is different from the asset being hedged. In cross hedging the optimal hedge ratio is given by equation (3.1).

Stock index futures are often used by portfolio managers. They can be used to hedge a portfolio so that the manager is out of the market for a period of time. Alternatively they can be used to change the beta of a portfolio. A short futures position reduces the beta of the portfolio; a long futures position increases the beta of a portfolio. The number of contracts that should be traded is the desired change in beta multiplied by the ratio of the value of the portfolio to the value of the assets underlying one contract. Note that a full hedge (giving the portfolio manager no exposure to the market) corresponds to changing the beta of the portfolio to zero. You should study Table 3.4 to make sure you understand how the capital asset pricing model works and how futures contracts can eliminate market risk.

The final part of the chapter discusses rolling hedges forward. This is a way of creating a hedge that lasts a relatively long time from short-dated futures contracts. The way hedges are rolled forward is as follows. You enter into a short-dated futures contract, close it out just before the delivery month, immediately replace it with another short-dated futures contract, close it out just before the delivery month, and so on. (Metallgesellschaft in Business Snapshot 3.2 illustrates potential problems in rolling a hedge forward.) It is worth noting that hedges created in this way do not qualify for hedge accounting the United States.

SOLUTIONS TO PRACTICE QUESTIONS

Problem 3.8.

In the Chicago Board of Trade's corn futures contract, the following delivery months are available: March, May, July, September, and December. State the contract that should be used for hedging when the expiration of the hedge is in

    a. June

    b. July

    c. January

A good rule of thumb is to choose a futures contract that has a delivery month as close as possible to, but later than, the month containing the expiration of the hedge. The contracts that should be used are therefore *See Pg 55 - 56 Text / Bottom Top*

(a) July

(b) September

(c) March

Problem 3.9.

Does a perfect hedge always succeed in locking in the current spot price of an asset for a future transaction? Explain your answer.

No. Consider, for example, the use of a forward contract to hedge a known cash inflow in a foreign currency. The forward contract locks in the forward exchange rate — which is in general different from the spot exchange rate.

Problem 3.10.

Explain why a short hedger's position improves when the basis strengthens unexpectedly and worsens when the basis weakens unexpectedly.

The basis is the amount by which the spot price exceeds the futures price. A short hedger is long the asset and short futures contracts. The value of his or her position therefore improves as the basis increases. Similarly it worsens as the basis decreases.

Problem 3.11.

Imagine you are the treasurer of a Japanese company exporting electronic equipment to the United States. Discuss how you would design a foreign exchange hedging strategy and the arguments you would use to sell the strategy to your fellow executives.

The simple answer to this question is that the treasurer should

1. Estimate the company's future cash flows in Japanese yen and U.S. dollars

2. Enter into forward and futures contracts to lock in the exchange rate for the U.S. dollar cash flows.

However, this is not the whole story. As the gold jewelry example in Table 3.1 shows, the company should examine whether the magnitudes of the foreign cash flows depend on the exchange rate. For example, will the company be able to raise the price of its product in U.S. dollars if the yen appreciates? If the company can do so, its foreign exchange exposure may be quite low. The key estimates required are those showing the overall effect on the company's profitability of changes in the exchange rate at various times in the future. Once these estimates have been produced the company can choose between using futures and options to hedge its risk. The results of the analysis should be presented carefully to other executives. It should be explained that a hedge does not ensure that profits will be higher. It means that profit will be more certain. When futures/forwards are used both the downside and upside are eliminated. With options a premium is paid to eliminate only the downside.

20 × 0.8
= 16 contracts
vs 20 contracts
if fully hedged.

Problem 3.12.

Suppose that in Example 3.4 the company decides to use a hedge ratio of 0.8. How does the decision affect the way in which the hedge is implemented and the result?

If the hedge ratio is 0.8, the company takes a long position in 16 NYM December oil futures contracts on June 8 when the futures price is $68.00. It closes out its position on November 10. The spot price and futures price at this time are $75.00 and $72. The gain on the futures position is

$$(72 - 68.00) \times 16,000 = 64,000$$

The effective cost of the oil is therefore

$$20,000 \times 75 - 64,000 = 1,436,000$$

or $71.80 per barrel. (This compares with $71.00 per barrel when the company is fully hedged.)

Problem 3.13.

"If the minimum-variance hedge ratio is calculated as 1.0, the hedge must be perfect." *Is this statement true? Explain your answer.*

The statement is not true. The minimum variance hedge ratio is

$$\rho \frac{\sigma_S}{\sigma_F}$$

It is 1.0 when $\rho = 0.5$ and $\sigma_S = 2\sigma_F$. Since $\rho < 1.0$ the hedge is clearly not perfect.

Problem 3.14.

"If there is no basis risk, the minimum variance hedge ratio is always 1.0." Is this statement true? Explain your answer.

The statement is true. Using the notation in the text, if the hedge ratio is 1.0, the hedger locks in a price of $F_1 + b_2$. Since both F_1 and b_2 are known this has a variance of zero and must be the best hedge.

Problem 3.15

"For an asset where futures prices are usually less than spot prices, long hedges are likely to be particularly attractive." Explain this statement.

A company that knows it will purchase a commodity in the future is able to lock in a price close to the futures price. This is likely to be particularly attractive when the futures price is less than the spot price. An illustration is provided by Example 3.2.

Problem 3.16.

The standard deviation of monthly changes in the spot price of live cattle is (in cents per pound) 1.2. The standard deviation of monthly changes in the futures price of live cattle for the closest contract is 1.4. The correlation between the futures price changes and the spot price changes is 0.7. It is now October 15. A beef producer is committed to purchasing 200,000 pounds of live cattle on November 15. The producer wants to use the December live-cattle futures contracts to hedge its risk. Each contract is for the delivery of 40,000 pounds of cattle. What strategy should the beef producer follow?

The optimal hedge ratio is

$$0.7 \times \frac{1.2}{1.4} = 0.6$$

The beef producer requires a long position in $200000 \times 0.6 = 120,000$ lbs of cattle. The beef producer should therefore take a long position in 3 December contracts closing out the position on November 15.

Problem 3.17.

A corn farmer argues "I do not use futures contracts for hedging. My real risk is not the price of corn. It is that my whole crop gets wiped out by the weather."Discuss this viewpoint. Should the farmer estimate his or her expected production of corn and hedge to try to lock in a price for expected production?

If weather creates a significant uncertainty about the volume of corn that will be harvested, the farmer should not enter into short forward contracts to hedge the price risk on his or her expected production. The reason is as follows. Suppose that the weather is bad and the farmer's production is lower than expected. Other farmers are likely to have been affected similarly. Corn production overall will be low and as a consequence the price of corn will be relatively high. The farmer's problems arising from the bad harvest will be made worse by losses on the short futures position. This problem emphasizes the importance of looking at the big picture when hedging. The farmer is correct to question whether hedging price risk while ignoring other risks is a good strategy.

Problem 3.18.

On July 1, an investor holds 50,000 shares of a certain stock. The market price is $30 per share. The investor is interested in hedging against movements in the market over the next month and decides to use the September Mini S&P 500 futures contract. The index is currently 1,500 and one contract is for delivery of $50 times the index. The beta of the stock is 1.3. What strategy should the investor follow? Under what circumstances will it be profitable?

A short position in

$$1.3 \times \frac{50,000 \times 30}{50 \times 1,500} = 26$$

contracts is required. It will be profitable if the stock outperforms the market in the sense that its return is greater than that predicted by the capital asset pricing model.

Problem 3.19.

Suppose that in Table 3.5 the company decides to use a hedge ratio of 1.5. How does the decision affect the way the hedge is implemented and the result?

17

If the company uses a hedge ratio of 1.5 in Table 3.5 it would at each stage short 150 contracts. The gain from the futures contracts would be

$$1.50 \times 1.70 = \$2.55 \text{ per barrel}$$

and the company would be \$0.85 per barrel better off.

Problem 3.20.

A futures contract is used for hedging. Explain why the daily settlement of the contract can give rise to cash flow problems.

Suppose that you enter into a short futures contract to hedge the sale of a asset in six months. If the price of the asset rises sharply during the six months, the futures price will also rise and you may get margin calls. The margin calls will lead to cash outflows. Eventually the cash outflows will be offset by the extra amount you get when you sell the asset, but there is a mismatch in the timing of the cash outflows and inflows. Your cash outflows occur earlier than your cash inflows. A similar situation could arise if you used a long position in a futures contract to hedge the purchase of an asset and the asset's price fell sharply. An extreme example of what we are talking about here is provided by Metallgesellschaft (see Business Snapshot 3.2).

Problem 3.21.

The expected return on the S&P 500 is 12% and the risk-free rate is 5%. What is the expected return on the investment with a beta of (a) 0.2, (b) 0.5, and (c) 1.4?

(a) $0.05 + 0.2 \times (0.12 - 0.05) = 0.064$ or 6.4%
(b) $0.05 + 0.5 \times (0.12 - 0.05) = 0.085$ or 8.5%
(c) $0.05 + 1.4 \times (0.12 - 0.05) = 0.148$ or 14.8%

CHAPTER 4
Interest Rates

This chapter provides background material on interest rates. Understanding this material is essential for the rest of the book. The chapter starts by discussing three interest rates that are important to derivatives markets: Treasury rates, LIBOR rates, and repo rates. Throughout the book we use the term "risk-free rate". For a derivatives trader short-term risk-free rates are LIBOR rates, not Treasury rates. This is explained in Business Snapshot 4.1. (As discussed in later chapters, Eurodollar futures quotes and swap rates are used to calculate risk-free rates for longer maturities.)

It is important that you understand the compounding frequency material in Section 4.2. It cannot be emphasized enough that the compounding frequency is nothing more than a unit of measurement. Consider two interest rates. One is 10% with semiannual compounding; the other is 10.25% with annual compounding. The interest rates are the same. They are just measured in different units. Converting an interest rate from one compounding frequency to another is like converting a distance from miles to kilometers. The concept of a continuously compounded interest rate is likely to be new to many readers. As we increase the compounding frequency when measuring interest rates, in the limit we get a unit of measurement known as continuous compounding. The formulas in options markets involve rates measured with continuous compounding and, except where otherwise stated, the rates in the book are measured with continuous compounding. It is therefore important that you make sure you become comfortable with continuously compounded rates. Equations (4.3) and (4.4) show how to convert a rate from a compounding frequency of m times per year to continuous compounding and vice versa. The appendix to the chapter provides a review of exponential and logarithmic functions for readers that need it.

The rates that are quoted in financial markets are often the rates corresponding to a situation where interest payments are made regularly (e.g., every six months). The rates important in derivatives markets are zero-coupon rates. These are the rates that correspond to a situation where money is invested at time 0 and all the return (interest and principal) is realized at some future time T. Plotting the zero rate as a function of the maturity T gives the zero-coupon term structure of interest rates. The discount rate that should be used for a cash flow occurring at time T is the zero-coupon interest rate for maturity T.

Two definitions should be noted. A bond yield is the discount rate for the cash flows on a bond (where the discount rate is assumed for this purpose to be the same for each cash flow) that causes the bond price to equal the market price. The par yield for a bond is the coupon rate that causes the bond price to equal its par value.

Section 4.5 describes a procedure for calculating Treasury zero rates from the rates on Treasury bills and Treasury bonds. Although not the most sophisticated procedure available, it is the one most widely used in practice. It is known as the bootstrap method. First

19

a short-term interest rate is determined from the shortest maturity instrument. Successively longer maturity instruments are then considered and used to calculate successively longer maturity rates.

Forward rates are the future rates of interest implied by zero-coupon interest rates. For example, if the one-year rate is 6% and the two-year rate is 8%, the forward rate for the second year is 10%. This is because 10% for the second year combined with 6% for the first year gives 8% for the two years. Note that this calculation is exact if the interest rates are measured with continuous compounding and only approximate when other compounding frequencies are used. A forward rate agreement (FRA) is an agreement that a certain interest rate will apply to a certain principal for a certain future time period. If the interest rate in the FRA is the forward rate, the value of the FRA is zero. Otherwise the value must be calculated using equations (4.9) and 4.10).

The chapter concludes by discussing the determinants of the term structure of interest rates. If market participants expect interest rates to rise in the future, the term structure will tend to be upward sloping and if market participants expect interest rates to fall it will tend to be downward sloping. However, as Section 4.8 points out this is not the whole story. There is a natural tendency for people to want to borrow for long periods of time and lend for short periods of time. In order to encourage more people to borrow for short periods and invest their money for long periods banks tend to raise the long-term interest rates they offer relative to the expectations of market participants.

SOLUTIONS TO PRACTICE QUESTIONS

Problem 4.8.

The cash prices of six-month and one-year Treasury bills are 94.0 and 89.0. A 1.5-year bond that will pay coupons of $4 every six months currently sells for $94.84. A two-year bond that will pay coupons of $5 every six months currently sells for $97.12. Calculate the six-month, one-year, 1.5-year, and two-year zero rates.

The 6-month Treasury bill provides a return of $6/94 = 6.383\%$ in six months. This is $2 \times 6.383 = 12.766\%$ per annum with semiannual compounding or $2\ln(1.06383) = 12.38\%$ per annum with continuous compounding. The 12-month rate is $11/89 = 12.360\%$ with annual compounding or $\ln(1.1236) = 11.65\%$ with continuous compounding.

For the $1\frac{1}{2}$ year bond we must have

$$4e^{-0.1238\times0.5} + 4e^{-0.1165\times1} + 104e^{-1.5R} = 94.84$$

where R is the $1\frac{1}{2}$ year zero rate. It follows that

$$3.76 + 3.56 + 104e^{-1.5R} = 94.84$$
$$e^{-1.5R} = 0.8415$$
$$R = 0.115$$

or 11.5%. For the 2-year bond we must have

$$5e^{-0.1238\times0.5} + 5e^{-0.1165\times1} + 5e^{-0.115\times1.5} + 105e^{-2R} = 97.12$$

20

$$4.70 + 4.45 + 4.2080 + 105e^{-2R} = 97.12$$
$$105e^{-2R} = 97.12 - 13.358 = 83.762$$
$$e^{-2R} = \frac{83.762}{105} = 0.7977$$

where R is the 2-year zero rate. It follows that

$$e^{-2R} = 0.7977$$
$$R = 0.113$$

$\ln(e^{-2R}) = \ln(.7977)$
$-2R = -.2260$
$R = \frac{.2260}{2} = .1130$

or 11.3%. ✓

Problem 4.9.

What rate of interest with continuous compounding is equivalent to 15% per annum with monthly compounding?

check later

$\left(1 + \frac{R}{12}\right)^{12} = 15$

The rate of interest is R where:

Page 83

$A \cdot e^{R \cdot n} = A\left(1 + \frac{R_m}{m}\right)^{mn}$

$e^{R \cdot n} = \left(1 + \frac{R_m}{m}\right)^{mn}$

i.e.,

if $n = 1$

$e^{R} = \left(1 + \frac{R_m}{m}\right)^{m}$

Before eq. 4.3, 4.4.

$$e^R = \left(1 + \frac{0.15}{12}\right)^{12}$$

Take $\ln$ of both sides

$$R = 12 \ln\left(1 + \frac{0.15}{12}\right)$$

$$= 0.1491$$

$\ln 15 = 12 \ln\left(1 + \frac{R}{12}\right)$
$\ln 15 = 12\left[\ln 1 + \ln R - \ln 12\right]$
$2.7081 = 12\left[0 + \ln R - 2.4849\right]$
$0.2257 + 2.4849 = \ln R$
$2.7106 = \ln R$ check

The rate of interest is therefore 14.91% per annum. ✓

14.91% with continuous compounding = 15% per annum with monthly compounding.

Problem 4.10.

$\left(1 + \frac{R}{12}\right)^{12} = 15$ ∴ $1 + \frac{R}{12} = 15^{\frac{1}{12}}$
$\frac{R}{12} = 15^{.0833} - 1 = 1.2531 - 1 = .2531$ $R = 3.0366$

A deposit account pays 12% per annum with continuous compounding, but interest is actually paid quarterly. How much interest will be paid each quarter on a $10,000 deposit?

The equivalent rate of interest with quarterly compounding is R where

$$e^{0.12} = \left(1 + \frac{R}{4}\right)^4$$

$e^{\frac{.12}{4}} = 1 + \frac{R}{4}$
$e^{.03} - 1 = \frac{R}{4}$

or

$$R = 4(e^{0.03} - 1) = 0.1218$$

$4(e^{.03} - 1) = R$
$4(1.0305 - 1) = R$
$4.1220 - 4 = R$
$.1220 = R$

The amount of interest paid each quarter is therefore:

$$10,000 \times \frac{0.1218}{4} = 304.55$$

$\left(10,000 \times e^{.12 \times .25}\right) - 10,000 = \$304.50$
$= 1.03045$

or $304.55.

Problem 4.11.

Suppose that 6-month, 12-month, 18-month, 24-month, and 30-month zero rates are 4%, 4.2%, 4.4%, 4.6%, and 4.8% per annum with continuous compounding respectively. Estimate the cash price of a bond with a face value of 100 that will mature in 30 months and pays a coupon of 4% per annum semiannually.

21

[handwritten top: 4% annual coupon]

The bond pays $2 in 6, 12, 18, and 24 months, and $102 in 30 months. The cash price
is *[handwritten: 4.2%]*

[handwritten above terms: 4% 4.4% 4.6%   4.8%]

$$2e^{-0.04\times0.5} + 2e^{-0.042\times1.0} + 2e^{-0.044\times1.5} + 2e^{-0.046\times2} + 102e^{-0.048\times2.5} = 98.04$$

[handwritten under terms: .9802 / .9589 / .9361 / .9121 / .8869]
[handwritten: =1.9604 + 1.9177 + 1.8722 + 1.8242 + 90.4638 = 98.04]
[handwritten above: -.10660 -.10920 -.11200]

Problem 4.12.

A three-year bond provides a coupon of 8% semiannually and has a cash price of 104.
What is the bond's yield?

[handwritten margin: × NO]

The bond pays $4 in 6, 12, 18, 24, and 30 months, and $104 in 36 months. The bond
yield is the value of y that solves

$$4e^{-0.5y} + 4e^{-1.0y} + 4e^{-1.5y} + 4e^{-2.0y} + 4e^{-2.5y} + 104e^{-3.0y} = 104$$

Using the *Goal Seek* tool in Excel $y = 0.06407$ or 6.407%.

Problem 4.13.

[handwritten above: 5%   6%   6.5%   7%]

Suppose that the 6-month, 12-month, 18-month, and 24-month zero rates are 5%, 6%,
6.5%, and 7% respectively. What is the two-year par yield?

[handwritten margin: see pgs. 85-86]

Using the notation in the text, $m = 2$, $d = e^{-0.07\times2} = 0.8694$. Also

[handwritten right: × d=e^{-zt} where z is 2 yr zero rate]

$$A = e^{-0.05\times0.5} + e^{-0.06\times1.0} + e^{-0.065\times1.5} + e^{-0.07\times2.0} = 3.6935$$

[handwritten under terms: .9753 .9418 .9071 .8694 = 3.6936]

The formula in the text gives the par yield as

[handwritten left: $c = \dfrac{(100 - 100d)m}{A}$ See Top of Pg. 86]

$$\frac{(100 - 100 \times 0.8694) \times 2}{3.6935} = 7.072$$

To verify that this is correct we calculate the value of a bond that pays a coupon of 7.072%
per year (that is 3.5365 every six months). The value is

[handwritten above terms: .9753   .9418   .9071   .8694]

$$3.536e^{-0.05\times0.5} + 3.5365e^{-0.06\times1.0} + 3.536e^{-0.065\times1.5} + 103.536e^{-0.07\times2.0} = 100$$

[handwritten under terms: 3.4487   3.3307   3.2075   90.01 = 99.9969]

verifying that 7.072% is the par yield.

Problem 4.14.

Suppose that zero interest rates with continuous compounding are as follows:

Maturity (years)	Rate (% per annum)
1	2.0
2	3.0
3	3.7
4	4.2
5	4.5

22

Page 89: Eqn. 4.6 $\quad R_F = R_2 + (R_2 - R_1)\dfrac{T_1}{T_2 - T_1}$

Calculate forward interest rates for the second, third, fourth, and fifth years.

The forward rates with continuous compounding are as follows:

Year 2:	4.0%	$\rightarrow R_F = 3 + (3-2)\dfrac{1}{2-1} = 4$
Year 3:	5.1%	$\rightarrow R_F = 3.7 + (3.7-3)\dfrac{2}{3-2} = 3.7 + 1.4 = 5.1$
Year 4:	5.7%	$\rightarrow R_F = 4.2 + (4.2-3.7)\dfrac{3}{4-3} = 4.2 + 1.5 = 5.7$
Year 5:	5.7%	$\rightarrow R_F = 4.5 + (4.5-4.2)\dfrac{4}{5-4} = 4.5 + 1.2 = 5.7\%$

Problem 4.15.

Use the rates in Problem 4.14 to value an FRA where you will pay 5% for the third year on $1 million.

The forward rate is 5.1% with continuous compounding or $e^{0.051 \times 1} - 1 = 5.232\%$ with annual compounding. The 3-year interest rate is 3.7% with continuous compounding. From equation (4.10), the value of the FRA is therefore

4.10 $\quad V_{FRA} = L(R_F - R_K)(T_2 - T_1)e^{-R_2 T_2}$

$$[1{,}000{,}000 \times (0.05232 - 0.05) \times 1]e^{-0.037 \times 3} = 2{,}078.85$$

$\underset{\text{Principal}}{L} \qquad R_F \qquad R_K \quad T_2 - T_1 \quad R_2 \; T_2$

or $1{,}964.67.

Problem 4.16.

A 10-year, 8% coupon bond currently sells for $90. A 10-year, 4% coupon bond currently sells for $80. What is the 10-year zero rate? (Hint: Consider taking a long position in two of the 4% coupon bonds and a short position in one of the 8% coupon bonds.)

Taking a long position in two of the 4% coupon bonds and a short position in one of the 8% coupon bonds leads to the following cash flows

Short Pₒₙ Receive   Payout on Long Pₒₙ (you are buying)

$$\text{Year } 0 : 90 - 2 \times 80 = -70$$

$$\text{Year } 10 : 200 - 100 = 100$$

on Long Pₒₙ   on Short Pₒₙ

because the coupons cancel out. $100 in 10 years time is equivalent to $70 today. The 10-year rate, R, (continuously compounded) is therefore given by

$$100 = 70e^{10R}$$

$\dfrac{100}{70} = e^{10R}$

$\ln\left(\dfrac{100}{70}\right) = \ln\left(e^{10R}\right)$

The rate is

$$\frac{1}{10}\ln\frac{100}{70} = 0.0357$$

$\ln\dfrac{100}{70} = 10R$

$\dfrac{1}{10} \cdot \ln\dfrac{100}{70} = \dfrac{.3567}{10}$

$R = \dfrac{1}{10} \cdot \ln\dfrac{100}{70}$

or 3.57% per annum.

$= .0357$

Problem 4.17.

Explain carefully why liquidity preference theory is consistent with the observation that the term structure of interest rates tends to be upward sloping more often than it is downward sloping.

If long-term rates were simply a reflection of expected future short-term rates, we would expect the term structure to be downward sloping as often as it is upward sloping. (This is based on the assumption that half of the time investors expect rates to increase and half of the time investors expect rates to decrease). Liquidity preference theory argues that long term rates are high relative to expected future short-term rates. This means that the term structure should be upward sloping more often than it is downward sloping.

Problem 4.18.

"When the zero curve is upward sloping, the zero rate for a particular maturity is greater than the par yield for that maturity. When the zero curve is downward sloping the reverse is true." Explain why this is so.

The par yield is the yield on a coupon-bearing bond. The zero rate is the yield on a zero-coupon bond. When the yield curve is upward sloping, the yield on an N-year coupon-bearing bond is less than the yield on an N-year zero-coupon bond. This is because the coupons are discounted at a lower rate than the N-year rate and drag the yield down below this rate. Similarly, when the yield curve is downward sloping, the yield on an N-year coupon bearing bond is higher than the yield on an N-year zero-coupon bond.

Problem 4.19.

Why are U.S. Treasury rates significantly lower than other rates that are close to risk free?

There are three reasons (see Business Snapshot 4.1).
1. Treasury bills and Treasury bonds must be purchased by financial institutions to fulfill a variety of regulatory requirements. This increases demand for these Treasury instruments driving the price up and the yield down.
2. The amount of capital a bank is required to hold to support an investment in Treasury bills and bonds is substantially smaller than the capital required to support a similar investment in other very-low-risk instruments.
3. In the United States, Treasury instruments are given a favorable tax treatment compared with most other fixed-income investments because they are not taxed at the state level.

Problem 4.20.

Why does a loan in the repo market involve very little credit risk?

A repo is a contract where an investment dealer who owns securities agrees to sell them to another company now and buy them back later at a slightly higher price. The other company is providing a loan to the investment dealer. This loan involves very little credit risk. If the borrower does not honor the agreement, the lending company simply keeps the securities. If the lending company does not keep to its side of the agreement, the original owner of the securities keeps the cash.

Problem 4.21.

Explain why an FRA is equivalent to the exchange of a floating rate of interest for a fixed rate of interest?

A FRA is an agreement that a certain specified interest rate, R_K, will apply to a certain principal, L, for a certain specified future time period. Suppose that the rate observed in the market for the future time period at the beginning of the time period proves to be R_M. If the FRA is an agreement that R_K will apply when the principal is invested, the holder of the FRA can borrow the principal at R_M and then invest it at R_K. The net cash flow at the end of the period is then an inflow of $R_K L$ and an outflow of $R_M L$. If the FRA is an agreement that R_K will apply when the principal is borrowed, the holder of the FRA can invest the borrowed principal at R_M. The net cash flow at the end of the period is then an inflow of $R_M L$ and an outflow of $R_K L$. In either case we see that the FRA involves the exchange of a fixed rate of interest on the principal of L for a floating rate of interest on the principal.

Problem 4.22.

"An interest rate swap where six-month LIBOR is exchanged for a fixed rate 5% on a principal of $100 million is a portfolio of FRAs." Explain.

Each exchange of payments is an FRA where interest at 5% is exchanged for interest at LIBOR on a principal of $100 million. Interest rate swaps are discussed further in Chapter 7.

CHAPTER 5
Determination of Forward and Futures Prices

This chapter explores the relationship between forward/futures prices and spot prices. An important distinction is between investment and consumption assets. Investment assets are assets held solely for investment by significant numbers of traders (not necessarily all traders). Consumption assets are assets that are held primarily for consumption.

Investment assets can be divided into three categories:
1. Those that provide no income (A Treasury bill falls into this category)
2. Those that provide a known cash income (A Treasury bond falls into this category)
3. Those that provide a known yield (Stock indices and foreign currencies fall into this category.)

For investment assets in the first category the relationship between the forward price and the spot price is given by equation (5.1); for those in the second category it is given by equation (5.2); for those in the third category it is given by equation (5.3). The relationships can be proved by no arbitrage arguments. If a forward price is higher than that the price given by equations (5.1) to (5.3), market participants will lock in a profit by shorting the forward contract and buying the asset. If the forward price is lower than this price, market participants will lock in a profit by doing the reverse: taking a long position in the forward contract and selling (or shorting) the asset.

The difference between the forward price of an asset and the value of a forward contract often causes confusion. The forward price of an asset for a particular maturity date is the delivery price that would be negotiated today for a forward contract with that maturity date. The value of a forward contract with a certain maturity date and a certain delivery price is the contract's economic value. When a forward contract is first entered into the value of the forward contract is zero and the delivery price is set equal to the forward price. As time goes by the forward price changes but the delivery price of the contract remains the same. The value of the contract is liable to become positive or negative. Equation (5.4) gives the value of a long forward contract in terms of the forward price. If you are still unclear about the difference between the forward price and the value of the forward contract, try Problem 5.9.

Futures prices are more difficult to determine than forward prices because of the daily settlement in futures contracts. However, it turns out that for most purposes the futures price for a contract with a certain maturity can be assumed to be the same as the forward price of a contract with that maturity. This means that equations (5.1) to (5.3) apply. A stock index is treated as an asset providing a yield equal to the dividend yield on the index. Equation (5.3) therefore applies with q equal to the average dividend yield on the index. A foreign currency is treated as an asset providing a yield equal to the foreign risk-free rate. It follows that in this instance equation (5.3) applies with q equal to the foreign risk-free rate. (See equation 5.9.)

For consumption commodities there is no exact relationship between the futures price and the spot prices. The relationship that exists for an investment asset provides an upper bound for consumption assets. If the futures price is above this upper bound an arbitrageur can short futures and buy the asset to lock in a profit. However, if the futures price is below the upper bound there is no arbitrage opportunity. This is because the asset is not held for investment purposes. As a result there may well be no traders who own the asset and are prepared to forego the opportunity to consume the asset by selling it and buying the futures contract. For consumption assets an important concept is the convenience yield. This is a measure of the amount by which the futures price is less than its upper bound. (See equation 5.17.)

The last part of the chapter discusses the relationship between futures prices and expected future spot prices. If the asset has no systematic risk, the futures price equals the expected future spot price. If the asset has positive systematic risk, the futures price understates the expected future spot price. If it has negative systematic risk, the futures price overstates the expected future spot price.

SOLUTIONS TO PRACTICE QUESTIONS

Problem 5.8.

Is the futures price of a stock index greater than or less than the expected future value of the index? Explain your answer.

The futures price of a stock index is always less than the expected future value of the index. This follows from Section 5.14 and the fact that the index has positive systematic risk. For an alternative argument, let μ be the expected return required by investors on the index so that $E(S_T) = S_0 e^{(\mu - q)T}$. Because $\mu > r$ and $F_0 = S_0 e^{(r-q)T}$, it follows that $E(S_T) > F_0$.

Problem 5.9.

A one-year long forward contract on a non-dividend-paying stock is entered into when the stock price is $40 and the risk-free rate of interest is 10% per annum with continuous compounding.

a. What are the forward price and the initial value of the forward contract?

b. Six months later, the price of the stock is $45 and the risk-free interest rate is still 10%. What are the forward price and the value of the forward contract?

(a) The forward price, F_0, is given by equation (5.1) as:

$$F_0 = 40e^{0.1 \times 1} = 44.21$$

$F_0 = S_0 e^{Rt}$ 5.1

Pg. 107

or $44.21. The initial value of the forward contract is zero.

(b) The delivery price K in the contract is $44.21. The value of the contract, f, after six months is given by equation (5.5) as:

$$f = 45 - 44.21e^{-0.1 \times 0.5}$$

$f = S_0 - Ke^{-RT}$

Value of a forward contract on an investment asset that provides no income

$$= 2.95$$

i.e., it is $2.95. The forward price is:

$$45e^{0.1 \times 0.5} = 47.31$$

or $47.31.

Problem 5.10.

The risk-free rate of interest is 7% per annum with continuous compounding, and the dividend yield on a stock index is 3.2% per annum. The current value of the index is 150. What is the six-month futures price?

Using equation (5.3) the six month futures price is

$$150e^{(0.07-0.032) \times 0.5} = 152.88$$

or $152.88.

Problem 5.11.

Assume that the risk-free interest rate is 9% per annum with continuous compounding and that the dividend yield on a stock index varies throughout the year. In February, May, August, and November, dividends are paid at a rate of 5% per annum. In other months, dividends are paid at a rate of 2% per annum. Suppose that the value of the index on July 31 is 1,300. What is the futures price for a contract deliverable on December 31 of the same year?

The futures contract lasts for five months. The dividend yield is 2% for three of the months and 5% for two of the months. The average dividend yield is therefore

$$\frac{1}{5}(3 \times 2 + 2 \times 5) = 3.2\%$$

The futures price is therefore

$$1300e^{(0.09-0.032) \times 0.4167} = 1,331.80$$

or $1331.80.

Problem 5.12.

Suppose that the risk-free interest rate is 10% per annum with continuous compounding and that the dividend yield on a stock index is 4% per annum. The index is standing at 400, and the futures price for a contract deliverable in four months is 405. What arbitrage opportunities does this create?

The theoretical futures price is

$$400e^{(0.10-0.04) \times 4/12} = 408.08$$

28

The actual futures price is only 405. This shows that the index futures price is too low relative to the index. The correct arbitrage strategy is

    1. Buy futures contracts

    2. Short the shares underlying the index.

Problem 5.13.

Estimate the difference between short-term interest rates in Japan and the United States on August 4, 2009 from the information in Table 5.4.

The settlement prices for the futures contracts are

Sep	1.0502
Dec	1.0512

Japanese Yen

The December 2009 price is about 0.0952% above the September 2009 price. This suggests that the short-term interest rate in the United States exceeded short-term interest rate in the United Japan by about 0.0952% per three months or about 0.38% per year.

Problem 5.14.

The two-month interest rates in Switzerland and the United States are 2% and 5% per annum, respectively, with continuous compounding. The spot price of the Swiss franc is $0.8000. The futures price for a contract deliverable in two months is $0.8100. What arbitrage opportunities does this create?

The theoretical futures price is

$r - q$ t *Compare*

$$0.8000e^{(0.05-0.02)\times 2/12} = 0.8040$$

The actual futures price is too high. This suggests that an arbitrageur should buy Swiss francs and short Swiss francs futures.

Problem 5.15.

The current price of silver is $15 per ounce. The storage costs are $0.24 per ounce per year payable quarterly in advance. Assuming that interest rates are 10% per annum for all maturities, calculate the futures price of silver for delivery in nine months.

$\$ .06$ *per quarter*

The present value of the storage costs for nine months are

$$0.06 + 0.06e^{-0.10\times 0.25} + 0.06e^{-0.10\times 0.5} = 0.176$$

Pay now   *Pay in 3 months*   *Pay in 6 months*

or $0.176. The futures price is from equation (5.11) given by F_0 where

r t

$$F_0 = (15.000 + 0.176)e^{0.1\times 0.75} = 16.36$$

9 months

i.e., it is $16.36 per ounce.

Problem 5.16.

Suppose that F_1 and F_2 are two futures contracts on the same commodity with times to maturity, t_1 and t_2, where $t_2 > t_1$. Prove that

$$F_2 \leq F_1 e^{r(t_2 - t_1)}$$

where r is the interest rate (assumed constant) and there are no storage costs. For the purposes of this problem, assume that a futures contract is the same as a forward contract.

If

$$F_2 > F_1 e^{r(t_2 - t_1)}$$

an investor could make a riskless profit by
  1. Taking a long position in a futures contract which matures at time t_1
  2. Taking a short position in a futures contract which matures at time t_2
When the first futures contract matures, the asset is purchased for F_1 using funds borrowed at rate r. It is then held until time t_2 at which point it is exchanged for F_2 under the second contract. The costs of the funds borrowed and accumulated interest at time t_2 is $F_1 e^{r(t_2 - t_1)}$ A positive profit of

$$F_2 - F_1 e^{r(t_2 - t_1)}$$

is then realized at time t_2. This type of arbitrage opportunity cannot exist for long. Hence:

$$F_2 \leq F_1 e^{r(t_2 - t_1)}$$

Problem 5.17.

When a known future cash outflow in a foreign currency is hedged by a company using a forward contract, there is no foreign exchange risk. When it is hedged using futures contracts, the daily settlement process does leave the company exposed to some risk. Explain the nature of this risk. In particular, consider whether the company is better off using a futures contract or a forward contract when

  a. The value of the foreign currency falls rapidly during the life of the contract
  b. The value of the foreign currency rises rapidly during the life of the contract
  c. The value of the foreign currency first rises and then falls back to its initial value
  d. The value of the foreign currency first falls and
  then rises back to its initial value

  Assume that the forward price equals the futures price.

In total the gain or loss under a futures contract is equal to the gain or loss under the corresponding forward contract. However the timing of the cash flows is different. When the time value of money is taken into account a futures contract may prove to be more valuable or less valuable than a forward contract. Of course the company does not know in advance which will work out better. The long forward contract provides a perfect hedge. The long futures contract provides a slightly imperfect hedge.

(a) In this case the forward contract would lead to a slightly better outcome. The company will make a loss on its hedge. If the hedge is with a forward contract the whole of the loss will be realized at the end. If it is with a futures contract the loss will be realized day by day throughout the contract. On a present value basis the former is preferable.

(b) In this case the futures contract would lead to a slightly better outcome. The company will make a gain on the hedge. If the hedge is with a forward contract the gain will be realized at the end. If it is with a futures contract the gain will be realized day by day throughout the life of the contract. On a present value basis the latter is preferable.

(c) In this case the futures contract would lead to a slightly better outcome. This is because it would involve positive cash flows early and negative cash flows later.

(d) In this case the forward contract would lead to a slightly better outcome. This is because, in the case of the futures contract, the early cash flows would be negative and the later cash flow would be positive.

Problem 5.18.

It is sometimes argued that a forward exchange rate is an unbiased predictor of future exchange rates. Under what circumstances is this so?

From the discussion in Section 5.14 of the text, the forward exchange rate is an unbiased predictor of the future exchange rate when the exchange rate has no systematic risk. To have no systematic risk the exchange rate must be uncorrelated with the return on the market.

Problem 5.19.

Show that the growth rate in an index futures price equals the excess return of the portfolio underlying the index over the risk-free rate. Assume that the risk-free interest rate and the dividend yield are constant.

Suppose that F_0 is the futures price at time zero for a contract maturing at time T and F_1 is the futures price for the same contract at time t_1. It follows that

$$F_0 = S_0 e^{(r-q)T}$$

$$F_1 = S_1 e^{(r-q)(T-t_1)}$$

where S_0 and S_1 are the spot price at times zero and t_1, r is the risk-free rate, and q is the dividend yield. These equations imply that

$$\frac{F_1}{F_0} = \frac{S_1}{S_0} e^{-(r-q)t_1}$$

Define the excess return of the portfolio underlying the index over the risk-free rate as x. The total return is $r + x$ and the return realized in the form of capital gains is $r + x - q$. It follows that $S_1 = S_0 e^{(r+x-q)t_1}$ and the equation for F_1/F_0 reduces to

$$\frac{F_1}{F_0} = e^{xt_1}$$

which is the required result.

Problem 5.20.

Show that equation (5.3) is true by considering an investment in the asset combined with a short position in a futures contract. Assume that all income from the asset is reinvested in the asset. Use an argument similar to that in footnotes 2 and 4 and explain in detail what an arbitrageur would do if equation (5.3) did not hold.

Suppose we buy N units of the asset and invest the income from the asset in the asset. The income from the asset causes our holding in the asset to grow at a continuously compounded rate q. By time T our holding has grown to Ne^{qT} units of the asset. Analogously to footnotes 2 and 4 of Chapter 5, we therefore buy N units of the asset at time zero at a cost of S_0 per unit and enter into a forward contract to sell Ne^{qT} unit for F_0 per unit at time T. This generates the following cash flows:

Time 0: $-NS_0$

Time T: NF_0e^{qT}

Because there is no uncertainty about these cash flows, the present value of the time T inflow must equal the time zero outflow when we discount at the risk-free rate. This means that

$$NS_0 = (NF_0e^{qT})e^{-rT}$$

or

$$F_0 = S_0e^{(r-q)T}$$

This is equation (5.3).

If $F_0 > S_0e^{(r-q)T}$, an arbitrageur should borrow money at rate r and buy N units of the asset. At the same time the arbitrageur should enter into a forward contract to sell Ne^{qT} units of the asset at time T. As income is received, it is reinvested in the asset. At time T the loan is repaid and the arbitrageur makes a profit of $N(F_0e^{qT} - S_0e^{rT})$ at time T.

If $F_0 < S_0e^{(r-q)T}$, an arbitrageur should short N units of the asset investing the proceeds at rate r. At the same time the arbitrageur should enter into a forward contract to buy Ne^{qT} units of the asset at time T. When income is paid on the asset, the arbitrageur owes money on the short position. The investor meets this obligation from the cash proceeds of shorting further units. The result is that the number of units shorted grows at rate q to Ne^{qT}. The cumulative short position is closed out at time T and the arbitrageur makes a profit of $N(S_0e^{rT} - F_0e^{qT})$.

Problem 5.21.

Explain carefully what is meant by the expected price of a commodity on a particular future date. Suppose that the futures price of crude oil declines with the maturity of the contract at the rate of 2% per year. Assume that speculators tend to be short crude oil futures and hedgers tended to be long crude oil futures. What does the Keynes and Hicks argument imply about the expected future price of oil?

To understand the meaning of the expected future price of a commodity, suppose that there are N different possible prices at a particular future time: $P_1, P_2, \ldots, P_N$. Define

32

q_i as the (subjective) probability the price being P_i (with $q_1 + q_2 + \ldots + q_N = 1$). The expected future price is

$$\sum_{i=1}^{N} q_i P_i$$

Different people may have different expected future prices for the commodity. The expected future price in the market can be thought of as an average of the opinions of different market participants. Of course, in practice the actual price of the commodity at the future time may prove to be higher or lower than the expected price.

Keynes and Hicks argue that speculators on average make money from commodity futures trading and hedgers on average lose money from commodity futures trading. If speculators tend to have short positions in crude oil futures, the Keynes and Hicks argument implies that futures prices overstate expected future spot prices. If crude oil futures prices decline at 2% per year the Keynes and Hicks argument therefore implies an even faster decline for the expected price of crude oil if speculators are short.

Problem 5.22.
The Value Line Index is designed to reflect changes in the value of a portfolio of over 1,600 equally weighted stocks. Prior to March 9, 1988, the change in the index from one day to the next was calculated as the *geometric* average of the changes in the prices of the stocks underlying the index. In these circumstances, does equation (5.8) correctly relate the futures price of the index to its cash price? If not, does the equation overstate or understate the futures price?

When the geometric average of the price relatives is used, the changes in the value of the index do not correspond to changes in the value of a portfolio that is traded. Equation (5.8) is therefore no longer correct. The changes in the value of the portfolio is monitored by an index calculated from the arithmetic average of the prices of the stocks in the portfolio. Since the geometric average of a set of numbers is always less than the arithmetic average, equation (5.8) overstates the futures price. It is rumored that at one time (prior to 1988), equation (5.8) did hold for the Value Line Index. A major Wall Street firm was the first to recognize that this represented a trading opportunity. It made a financial killing by buying the stocks underlying the index and shorting the futures.

CHAPTER 6
Interest Rate Futures

This chapter discusses how interest rate futures work and how they are used for hedging. To understand the way interest rate futures are quoted it is necessary to understand day count conventions. The day count convention defines the number of days that the interest rate applies to and the way in which the interest earned accrues through time. Actual/Actual in period, 30/360, and Actual/360 are popular day count conventions in the United States. Look at Business Snapshot 6.1 and Problem 6.19 to check that you understand how Actual/Actual in period (which applies to Treasury bonds) and 30/360 (which applies to corporate bonds) work.

The most important long-term Treasury bond futures contracts in the United States are the Treasury bond and Treasury note futures contracts. These have some interesting delivery arrangements. In the case of the Treasury bond futures contract, any Treasury bond with a maturity of at least 15 years and not callable within 15 years can be delivered. In the case of the Treasury note futures contract, any Treasury bond with a maturity of between $6\frac{1}{2}$ and 10 years can be delivered. (The party with the short position chooses which bond will be delivered and when during the delivery month it will be delivered.) To calculate how much is paid and received for the bond the most recent futures prices is multiplied by a conversion factor and there is then an adjustment for accruals. Roughly speaking, the conversion factor is the price the bond would have if the zero-coupon yield curve were flat a 6%. Traders, who hold short futures positions and want to make delivery, typically look at all the different bonds that can be delivered and calculate a cheapest-to-deliver bond.

The most important short-term futures contracts in the United States are the three-month Eurodollar futures contracts. These contracts trade with delivery months as much as 10 years in the future. The underlying in a three-month Eurodollar futures contract is 100 minus the three-month LIBOR percentage rate of interest. The contract is settled in cash. It is marked to market daily until the third Wednesday of the delivery month. At that time the settlement price is calculated as 100 minus the three-month LIBOR percentage rate observed in the market. A futures contract is structured so that when the futures quote increases by one basis point (e.g. from 95.22 to 95.23) there is a gain of $25 on one long contract.

Because Eurodollar futures contracts are so liquid analysts often use them to estimate forward interest rates. Suppose that the December 2015 Eurodollar futures price is 95.00. Does this mean that (with the appropriate compounding frequency and day count conventions) the forward rate for a three month period beginning on the third Wednesday of December 2015 is 100–95.00 or 5.00%? The answer is that is necessary to make what is termed a "convexity adjustment" to convert the 5.00% to the required forward rate. The convexity adjustment is described in Section 6.3. It increases as the maturity of the futures contract increases. In the example considered in the text it increases from 0 to 73.8 basis points as the contract maturity increases from 0 to 10 years. (See Table 6.2.)

The last part of the chapter covers duration. The duration of an instrument describes its sensitivity to interest rates. Specifically it describes the sensitivity to a small parallel shift in the yield curve. The key equation is equation (6.7) when interest rates are expressed with continuous compounding and equation (6.9) when interest rates are expressed with a compounding frequency of m times per year. Suppose that the duration of an instrument is 4 years and we are considering the effect of a 0.05% increase in all interest rates. In this case $D = 4$ and $\Delta y = 0.0005$. Equation (6.7) shows that change in the price of the instrument being considered is 4×0.0005 or 0.002 times the price. This means that the percentage change is 0.2%.

When hedging an interest rate exposure using a futures contract the hedge ratio is determined by a) the duration of the instrument underlying the futures contract at the contract maturity and b) the duration of the exposure being hedged at the contract maturity. For example if the duration of the bond that is expected to be delivered in a Treasury note futures contract is 8 years and the duration of the exposure that is being hedged is 12 years, the hedge ratio should be 1.5; that is the size of the futures position should be 50% greater than the size of the position being hedged. (See equation 6.10.)

SOLUTIONS TO PRACTICE QUESTIONS

Problem 6.8.

% annual interest rate.

The price of a 90-day Treasury bill is quoted as 10.00. What continuously compounded return (on an actual/365 basis) does an investor earn on the Treasury bill for the 90-day period?

The cash price of the Treasury bill is

$$\frac{10}{4} = 2.5$$

$$100 - \left(\frac{90}{360} \times 10\right) = \$97.50$$

The annualized continuously compounded return is

$$\left(1 + \frac{2.5}{97.5}\right)^{365/90}$$

$$\frac{365}{90} \ln\left(1 + \frac{2.5}{97.5}\right) = 10.27\%$$

$= .0256$

$\ln 1.0256$
$= .0253$

$\frac{365}{90} \ln\left(1 + \frac{2.5}{97.5}\right)$

$= 4.0556$ See Pg 23 Prob. 4.16 for similar example.

$100 - 2.5 = 97.5$

$4.0556(.0253)$
$= .1025$
$= 10.27\%$

Problem 6.9.

It is May 5, 2010. The quoted price of a government bond with a 12% coupon that matures on July 27, 2014, is 110-17. What is the cash price?

The number of days between January 27, 2010 and May 5, 2010 is 98. The number of days between January 27, 2010 and July 27, 2010 is 181. The accrued interest is therefore

12% annual compan
$= 6\%$ semi annual

$$6 \times \frac{98}{181} = 3.2486$$

Jan 4
Feb 28
Mar 31
Apr 30
May 5
98

The quoted price is 110.5312. The cash price is therefore

$110 \frac{17}{32}$
$= 110.5312$

$$110.5312 + 3.2486 = 113.7798$$

Quoted Price   Accrued Interest

35

or $113.78.

Problem 6.10.

Suppose that the Treasury bond futures price is 101-12. Which of the following four bonds is cheapest to deliver?

$\frac{12}{32} = .3750$

Bond	Price	Conversion Factor
1	125-05	1.2131
2	142-15	1.3792
3	115-31	1.1149
4	144-02	1.4026

The cheapest-to-deliver bond is the one for which

$$\text{Quoted Price} - \text{Futures Price} \times \text{Conversion Factor}$$

is least. Calculating this factor for each of the 4 bonds we get

Bond 1: $125.15625 - (101.375 \times 1.2131) = 2.178$ *122.9780*

Bond 2: $142.46875 - (101.375 \times 1.3792) = 2.652$

Bond 3: $115.96875 - (101.375 \times 1.1149) = 2.946$

Bond 4: $144.06250 - (101.375 \times 1.4026) = 1.874$ *Cheapest*

Bond 4 is therefore the cheapest to deliver.

Problem 6.11. *drop*

It is July 30, 2012. The cheapest-to-deliver bond in a September 2012 Treasury bond futures contract is a 13% coupon bond, and delivery is expected to be made on September 30, 2012. Coupon payments on the bond are made on February 4 and August 4 each year. The term structure is flat, and the rate of interest with semiannual compounding is 12% per annum. The conversion factor for the bond is 1.5. The current quoted bond price is $110. Calculate the quoted futures price for the contract.

There are 176 days between February 4 and July 30 and 181 days between February 4 and August 4. The cash price of the bond is, therefore:

13% Coupon

$$110 + \left(\frac{176}{181} \times 6.5\right) = 116.32$$

$$\left(1 + \frac{.12}{2}\right)^2 = 2 \ln 1.06$$

.9724 × 6.5 = 6.3204

The rate of interest with continuous compounding is $2 \ln 1.06 = 0.1165$ or 11.65% per annum. A coupon of 6.5 will be received in 5 days ($= 0.01366$ years) time. The present value of the coupon is

$$6.5 e^{-0.01366 \times 0.1165} = 6.490$$

= 0.99841   *6.48967*

$\frac{5}{365} = .0137$

36

ln 1.06 = .0583
× 2
.1166

1 The futures contract lasts for 62 days (= 0.1694 years). The cash futures price if the contract were written on the 13% bond would be *(handwritten: given)*

(handwritten right: .1694 × .1165 = .01974 $e^{.01974} = 1.01993$)

$$(116.32 - 6.490)e^{0.1694 \times 0.1165} = 112.02$$

(handwritten: = 109.83   t   12)

At delivery there are 57 days of accrued interest. The quoted futures price if the contract were written on the 13% bond would therefore be

$$112.02 - 6.5 \times \frac{57}{184} = 110.01$$

(handwritten: $\frac{.13}{2}$ = .30978 × 6.5 = 2.01359   112.02 − 2.01359 = 110.01)

Taking the conversion factor into account the quoted futures price should be:

$$\frac{110.01}{1.5} = 73.34$$

(handwritten: given)

Problem 6.12.

An investor is looking for arbitrage opportunities in the Treasury bond futures market. What complications are created by the fact that the party with a short position can choose to deliver any bond with a maturity of over 15 years?

If the bond to be delivered and the time of delivery were known, arbitrage would be straightforward. When the futures price is too high, the arbitrageur buys bonds and shorts an equivalent number of bond futures contracts. When the futures price is too low, the arbitrageur shorts bonds and goes long an equivalent number of bond futures contracts.

Uncertainty as to which bond will be delivered introduces complications. The bond that appears cheapest-to-deliver now may not in fact be cheapest-to-deliver at maturity. In the case where the futures price is too high, this is not a major problem since the party with the short position (i.e., the arbitrageur) determines which bond is to be delivered. In the case where the futures price is too low, the arbitrageur's position is far more difficult since he or she does not know which bond to short; it is unlikely that a profit can be locked in for all possible outcomes.

Problem 6.13.

(handwritten: Given Libor 9 month 8% per annum   6 month 7.5% per annum)

Suppose that the nine-month LIBOR interest rate is 8% per annum and the six-month LIBOR interest rate is 7.5% per annum (both with actual/365 and continuous compounding). Estimate the three-month Eurodollar futures price quote for a contract maturing in six months.

(handwritten: 3 month)

The forward interest rate for the time period between months 6 and 9 is 9% per annum with continuous compounding. This is because 9% per annum for three months when combined with $7\frac{1}{2}$% per annum for six months gives an average interest rate of 8% per annum for the nine-month period.

(handwritten: Check)

With quarterly compounding the forward interest rate is

(handwritten: 3 month rate = 9%   6 month rate = $7\frac{1}{2}$%)

$$4(e^{0.09/4} - 1) = 0.09102$$

(handwritten right: Eqn 4.5 $\frac{R_2 \quad T_2 \qquad R_1}{(.08 \times .75) - (.075 \times}$ $\frac{.75 - .5}{T_2 \quad T_1}$ $\frac{.06 - .0375}{.25}$ =)

(handwritten bottom: $(e^{.09 \times .25})(1 + e^{.075 \times .5}) - 1 =$ 1.02276   1.0383)

or 9.102%. This assumes that the day count is actual/actual. With a day count of actual/360 the rate is $9.102 \times 360/365 = 8.977$. The three-month Eurodollar quote for a contract maturing in six months is therefore

$$100 - 8.977 = 91.02$$

Problem 6.14.

A five-year bond with a yield of 11% (continuously compounded) pays an 8% coupon at the end of each year.

a. What is the bond's price?
b. What is the bond's duration?
c. Use the duration to calculate the effect on the bond's price of a 0.2% decrease in its yield. $11 - .02 = 10.8\%$
d. Recalculate the bond's price on the basis of a (10.8%) per annum yield and verify that the result is in agreement with your answer to (c).

(a) The bond's price is

$$8e^{-0.11} + 8e^{-0.11\times2} + 8e^{-0.11\times3} + 8e^{-0.11\times4} + 108e^{-0.11\times5} = 86.80$$

[handwritten above terms: 7.16667 6.42015 5.75139 5.15229 62.31058]
[handwritten below terms: =.89583 .80252 .71892 .64404 .57695]

(b) The bond's duration is

$$\frac{1}{86.80}\left[8e^{-0.11} + 2\times8e^{-0.11\times2} + 3\times8e^{-0.11\times3} + 4\times8e^{-0.11\times4} + 5\times108e^{-0.11\times5}\right]$$

[handwritten below terms: 7.16667 12.84030 17.25417 20.60916 311.55290]

$$\frac{369.42320}{86.80} = 4.256 \text{ yrs} = 4.256 \text{ years}$$

(c) Since, with the notation in the chapter

$$\Delta B = -BD\Delta y$$

the effect on the bond's price of a 0.2% decrease in its yield is

$$86.80 \times 4.256 \times 0.002 = 0.74$$

[handwritten: + 86.80]

The bond's price should increase from 86.80 to 87.54.

(d) With a 10.8% yield the bond's price is

$$8e^{-0.108} + 8e^{-0.108\times2} + 8e^{-0.108\times3} + 8e^{-0.108\times4} + 108e^{-0.108\times5} = 87.54$$

[handwritten above terms: 7.18102 6.44588 5.78600 5.19368 62.93681]
[handwritten below terms: .89763 .80574 .72325 .64921 .58275]

This is consistent with the answer in (c).

Problem 6.15.

Suppose that a bond portfolio with a duration of 12 years is hedged using a futures contract in which the underlying asset has a duration of four years. What is likely to be the impact on the hedge of the fact that the 12-year rate is less volatile than the four-year rate?

Duration-based hedging procedures assume parallel shifts in the yield curve. Since the 12-year rate tends to move by less than the 4-year rate, the portfolio manager may find that he or she is over-hedged.

Problem 6.16.

Suppose that it is February 20 and a treasurer realizes that on July 17 the company will have to issue $5 million of commercial paper with a maturity of 180 days. If the paper were issued today, the company would realize $4,820,000. (In other words, the company would receive $4,820,000 for its paper and have to redeem it at $5,000,000 in 180 days' time.) The September Eurodollar futures price is quoted as 92.00. How should the treasurer hedge the company's exposure?

The company treasurer can hedge the company's exposure by shorting Eurodollar futures contracts. The Eurodollar futures position leads to a profit if rates rise and a loss if they fall. (prices rise)   180 days   Prices fall

The duration of the commercial paper is twice that of the Eurodollar deposit underlying the Eurodollar futures contract. The contract price of a Eurodollar futures contract is 980,000. The number of contracts that should be shorted is, therefore, Check

$$\frac{4,820,000}{980,000} \times 2 = 9.84$$

Rounding to the nearest whole number 10 contracts should be shorted.

Problem 6.17.

On August 1 a portfolio manager has a bond portfolio worth $10 million. The duration of the portfolio in October will be 7.1 years. The December Treasury bond futures price is currently 91-12 and the cheapest-to-deliver bond will have a duration of 8.8 years at maturity. How should the portfolio manager immunize the portfolio against changes in interest rates over the next two months?

The treasurer should short Treasury bond futures contract. If bond prices go down, this futures position will provide offsetting gains. The number of contracts that should be shorted is

$91 \frac{12}{32}$

$= 91.375$

$$\frac{10,000,000 \times 7.1}{91,375 \times 8.8} = 88.30$$

Rounding to the nearest whole number 88 contracts should be shorted.

Problem 6.18.

How can the portfolio manager change the duration of the portfolio to 3.0 years in Problem 6.17?

The answer in Problem 6.17 is designed to reduce the duration to zero. To reduce the duration from 7.1 to 3.0 instead of from 7.1 to 0, the treasurer should short

$7.1 - 3 = 4.1$

$$\frac{4.1}{7.1} \times 88.30 = 50.99$$

39

or 51 contracts.

Problem 6.19.

Between October 30, 2012, and November 1, 2012, you have a choice between owning a U.S. government bond paying a 12% coupon and a U.S. corporate bond paying a 12% coupon. Consider carefully the day count conventions discussed in this chapter and decide which of the two bonds you would prefer to own. Ignore the risk of default.

You would prefer to own the Treasury bond. Under the 30/360 day count convention there is one day between October 30 and November 1. Under the actual/actual (in period) day count convention, there are two days. Therefore you would earn approximately twice as much interest by holding the Treasury bond.

Problem 6.20.

Suppose that a Eurodollar futures quote is 88 for a contract maturing in 60 days. What is the LIBOR forward rate for the 60- to 150-day period? Ignore the difference between futures and forwards for the purposes of this question.

100−88=12

The Eurodollar futures contract price of 88 means that the Eurodollar futures rate is 12% per annum with quarterly compounding. This is the forward rate for the 60- to 150-day period with quarterly compounding and an actual/360 day count convention.

Problem 6.21.

The three-month Eurodollar futures price for a contract maturing in six years is quoted as 95.20. The standard deviation of the change in the short-term interest rate in one year is 1.1%. Estimate the forward LIBOR interest rate for the period between 6.00 and 6.25 years in the future.

Check

Using the notation of Section 6.3, $\sigma = 0.011$, $t_1 = 6$, and $t_2 = 6.25$. The convexity adjustment is

given

$$\frac{1}{2} \times 0.011^2 \times 6 \times 6.25 = 0.002269 = 23 \text{ basis points}$$

or about 23 basis points. The futures rate is 4.8% with quarterly compounding and an actual/360 day count. This becomes $4.8 \times 365/360 = 4.867\%$ with an actual/actual day count. It is $4\ln(1 + .04867/4) = 4.84\%$ with continuous compounding. The forward rate is therefore $4.84 - 0.23 = 4.61\%$ with continuous compounding.

Forward rate < futures rate

Problem 6.22.

Explain why the forward interest rate is less than the corresponding futures interest rate calculated from a Eurodollar futures contract.

Suppose that the contracts apply to the interest rate between times T_1 and T_2. There are two reasons for a difference between the forward rate and the futures rate. The first is that the futures contract is settled daily whereas the forward contract is settled once at time T_2. The second is that without daily settlement a futures contract would be settled at time T_1 not T_2. Both reasons tend to make the futures rate greater than the forward rate.

40

CHAPTER 7
Swaps

This chapter covers how interest rate swaps and currency swaps work and how they are valued. A plain vanilla interest rate swap is an agreement to exchange interest at a fixed rate for interest at LIBOR. Table 7.1 provides an example of a three-year swap where 5% is paid and six-month LIBOR is received with payments being exchanged every six months. The exchange made on September 5, 2010 is known on March 5, 2010 when the swap is initiated. The other exchanges depend on the LIBOR rates at future times. Note that the six-month LIBOR rate observed on a date determines the cash flows exchanged six months later.

An interest rate swap can be used to transform an asset or a liability. (See Example 7.1.) A swap where fixed is received and floating is paid can be used to convert a liability where a company is paying a fixed rate of interest to one where it is paying a floating rate of interest. The same swap can be used to convert an asset earning a floating rate of interest to an asset earning a fixed rate of interest. A swap where floating is received and fixed is paid can be used to convert a liability where a company is paying a floating rate of interest to one where it is paying a fixed rate of interest. The same swap can be used to convert an asset earning a fixed rate of interest to an asset earning a floating rate of interest. This is illustrated in Figures 7.2 and 7.3 where Microsoft and Intel trade with each other without a financial intermediary being involved and in Figures 7.4 and 7.5 where an intermediary is involved.

You should make sure you understand Table 7.3 and Business Snapshot 7.1. Table 7.3 shows quotes as they might be made by a swap market maker such as Goldman Sachs and Business Snapshot 7.1 shows an extract from a hypothetical swap confirmation.

The comparative advantage argument is sometimes used in an attempt to persuade corporate treasurers to enter into swaps. It is a superficially compelling argument. It says that companies should borrow in the market where they have a comparative advantage (AAA-rated companies should borrow at a fixed rate of interest; BBB-rated companies should borrow at a floating rate of interest). They should then use swaps to exchange the liability for what they want. In the case of fixed-for-fixed currency swaps, as discussed in Section 7.8, this type of argument can have some validity. However, in the case of interest rate swaps it is seriously flawed because it ignores the possibility of a company's creditworthiness declining so that the spread over LIBOR at which it borrows increases.

Section 7.5 shows that a swap rate is a low-credit-risk interest rate. For example the five-year swap rate corresponds to the rate earned by a financial institution when it lends a certain sum for six-months to an AA-rated companies and then relends it for nine further six-month periods ensuring that in each case the borrower has an AA-rating at the beginning of the six-month period. (You should make sure you understand why the five-year swap rate is less than the five-year borrowing rate for an AA-rated company.) Section 7.6 discusses how LIBOR deposit rates, Eurodollar futures quotes, and swap rates are used in the construction of the LIBOR/swap zero curve. Banks and other financial institutions calculate this zero curve at least once a day and use it as their risk-free zero curve. (As pointed out in Chapter 4 they do not use the Treasury zero curve as the risk-free zero curve.)

You should understand both ways of valuing interest rate swaps listed in Section 7.7. An interest rate swap can be regarded as the exchange of a bond paying LIBOR for a bond paying a fixed rate of interest. It can also be regarded as a portfolio of forward rate agreements (FRAs). Valuing an interest rate swap as a portfolio of forward rate agreements involves calculating the cash flows on the assumption that forward LIBOR interest rates are realized and then discounting the cash flows at the swap/LIBOR zero rates. Examples 7.4 and 7.5 illustrate the two approaches.

A fixed-for-fixed currency swap is an agreement to exchange a fixed rate in one currency for a fixed rate in another currency. It can be used to transform borrowings in one currency to borrowings in another currency or to transform an asset earning interest in one currency to an asset earning interest in another currency. Similarly to an interest rate swap, a currency swap can be valued either in terms on bonds or in terms of forward foreign exchange agreements. Examples 7.6 and 7.7 illustrate this.

Swap transactions entail a small amount of credit risk. A swap has zero value when it is first negotiated. As time passes its value is liable to become positive or negative. The credit exposure of a company (i.e., the amount it could lose if the counterparty defaults) is $\max(V, 0)$ where V is the value of the swap (see Figure 7.14). Part of the spread earned by a swap market marker (see Table 7.3) is to compensate for potential defaults by its counterparties.

Many different types of swaps are traded in practice. The final section of the chapter introduces you to some of the more important swap products.

SOLUTIONS TO PRACTICE QUESTIONS

Problem 7.8.
Explain why a bank is subject to credit risk when it enters into two offsetting swap contracts.

At the start of the swap, both contracts have a value of approximately zero. As time passes, it is likely that the swap values will change, so that one swap has a positive value to the bank and the other has a negative value to the bank. If the counterparty on the other side of the positive-value swap defaults, the bank still has to honor its contract with the other counterparty. It is liable to lose an amount equal to the positive value of the swap.

Problem 7.9.
Companies X and Y have been offered the following rates per annum on a $5 million 10-year investment:

	Fixed Rate	Floating Rate
Company X Wants fixed	8.0%	LIBOR
Company Y Wants floating	8.8%	LIBOR

0.8% spread

Company X requires a fixed-rate investment; company Y requires a floating-rate investment. Design a swap that will net a bank, acting as intermediary, 0.2% per annum and will appear equally attractive to X and Y.

The spread between the interest rates offered to X and Y is 0.8% per annum on fixed rate investments and 0.0% per annum on floating rate investments. This means that the total apparent benefit to all parties from the swap is 0.8% per annum. Of this 0.2% per annum will go to the bank. This leaves 0.3% per annum for each of X and Y. In other words, company X should be able to get a fixed-rate return of 8.3% per annum while company Y should be able to get a floating-rate return LIBOR + 0.3% per annum. The required swap is shown in Figure S7.1. The bank earns 0.2%, company X earns 8.3%, and company Y earns LIBOR + 0.3%.

Bank Pays

Figure S7.1   Swap for Problem 7.9

X

+ Libor
− Libor
+ 8.3
_____
8.3

Bank
+ 8.5
− 8.3
+ Libor
− Libor = + 0.2

+ 8.8%
− 8.5%
+ Libor
_____
Libor + 0.3%

Problem 7.10.

A financial institution has entered into an interest rate swap with company X. Under the terms of the swap, it receives 10% per annum and pays six-month LIBOR on a principal of $10 million for five years. Payments are made every six months. Suppose that company X defaults on the sixth payment date (end of year 3) when the interest rate (with semiannual compounding) is 8% per annum for all maturities. What is the loss to the financial institution? Assume that six-month LIBOR was 9% per annum halfway through year 3.

At the end of year 3 the financial institution was due to receive $500,000 (= 0.5 × 10% of $10 million) and pay $450,000 (= 0.5 × 9% of $10 million). The immediate loss is therefore $50,000. To value the remaining swap we assume than forward rates are realized. All forward rates are 8% per annum. The remaining cash flows are therefore valued on the assumption that the floating payment is $0.5 \times 0.08 \times 10,000,000 = \$400,000$ and the net payment that would be received is $500,000 - 400,000 = \$100,000$. The total cost of default is therefore the cost of foregoing the following cash flows:

43

year 3: $50,000   50,000 → 50,500 $e^{-.04 \times 1}$

year $3\frac{1}{2}$: $100,000 ÷ 1.04 — 96,153.85 → 96,078.94 $e^{-.04 \times 2}$

year 4: $100,000 ÷ 1.04^2 → 92,455.62 → 92,311.63 $e^{-.04 \times 2}$

year $4\frac{1}{2}$: $100,000 ÷ 1.04^3 → 88,899.64 → 88,692.04 $e^{-.04 \times 3}$

year 5: $100,000 ÷ 1.04^4 → 85,480.42 → 85,214.38 $e^{-.04 \times 4}$

Discounting these cash flows to year 3 at 4% per six months we obtain the cost of the default as $413,000.

     412,989.559   412,296.99

Problem 7.11.

A financial institution has entered into a 10-year currency swap with company Y. Under the terms of the swap, the financial institution receives interest at 3% per annum in Swiss francs and pays interest at 8% per annum in U.S. dollars. Interest payments are exchanged once a year. The principal amounts are 7 million dollars and 10 million francs. Suppose that company Y declares bankruptcy at the end of year 6, when the exchange rate is $0.80 per franc. What is the cost to the financial institution? Assume that, at the end of year 6, the interest rate is 3% per annum in Swiss francs and 8% per annum in U.S. dollars for all maturities. All interest rates are quoted with annual compounding.

When interest rates are compounded annually

$7 million   10 mill Francs   × .03   300,000 Franc int rec'd

.08 $560,000 Pd int pd.

$$F_0 = S_0 \left(\frac{1+r}{1+r_f} \right)^T$$

where F_0 is the T-year forward rate, S_0 is the spot rate, r is the domestic risk-free rate, and r_f is the foreign risk-free rate. As $r = 0.08$ and $r_f = 0.03$, the spot and forward exchange rates at the end of year 6 are

spot: 0.8000 $.80 \left(\frac{1+.08}{1+.03} \right) = .83883$ 1 yr forw

1 year forward: 0.8388 $.80 \left(\frac{1.08}{1.03} \right)^2 \approx .87956$ 2 yr forward

2 year forward: 0.8796 $.92225$ 3 yr fwd

3 year forward: 0.9223 $.80 \left(\frac{1.08}{1.03} \right)^3 \approx$

4 year forward: 0.9670 $.80 \left(\frac{1.08}{1.03} \right)^4 = .9670$ 4 yr forward

The value of the swap at the time of the default can be calculated on the assumption that forward rates are realized. The cash flows lost as a result of the default are therefore as follows:

Year	Dollar Paid	Swiss Franc Received	Forward Rate	Dollar Equivalent of Swiss Franc Received	Cash Flow Lost
6	560,000	300,000	0.8000	240,000	(320,000)
7	560,000	300,000	0.8388	251,600	(308,400)
8	560,000	300,000	0.8796	263,900	(296,100)
9	560,000	300,000	0.9223	276,700	(283,300)
10	7,560,000	10,300,000	0.9670	9,960,100	2,400,100

Discounting the numbers in the final column to the end of year 6 at 8% per annum, the cost of the default is $679,800.

44

Note that, if this were the only contract entered into by company Y, it would make no sense for the company to default at the end of year six as the exchange of payments at that time has a positive value to company Y. In practice company Y is likely to be defaulting and declaring bankruptcy for reasons unrelated to this particular contract and payments on the contract are likely to stop when bankruptcy is declared.

Problem 7.12.

Companies A and B face the following interest rates (adjusted for the differential impact of taxes):

	A *Wants US $ Floating*	B *Wants Canad in Fixed diff*	
U.S. dollars (floating rate)	LIBOR + 0.5%	LIBOR + 1.0%	0.5%
Canadian dollars (fixed rate)	5.0% *A Advantage*	6.5% *B's advantage*	1.5%

Assume that A wants to borrow U.S. dollars at a floating rate of interest and B wants to borrow Canadian dollars at a fixed rate of interest. A financial institution is planning to arrange a swap and requires a 50-basis-point spread. If the swap is equally attractive to A and B, what rates of interest will A and B end up paying?

Company A has a comparative advantage in the Canadian dollar fixed-rate market. Company B has a comparative advantage in the U.S. dollar floating-rate market. (This may be because of their tax positions.) However, company A wants to borrow in the U.S. dollar floating-rate market and company B wants to borrow in the Canadian dollar fixed-rate market. This gives rise to the swap opportunity.

The differential between the U.S. dollar floating rates is 0.5% per annum, and the differential between the Canadian dollar fixed rates is 1.5% per annum. The difference between the differentials is 1% per annum. The total potential gain to all parties from the swap is therefore 1% per annum, or 100 basis points. If the financial intermediary requires 50 basis points, each of A and B can be made 25 basis points better off. Thus a swap can be designed so that it provides A with U.S. dollars at LIBOR + 0.25% per annum, and B with Canadian dollars at 6.25% per annum. The swap is shown in Figure S7.2.

(margin handwriting: 1.5 / −0.5 / 1.0)

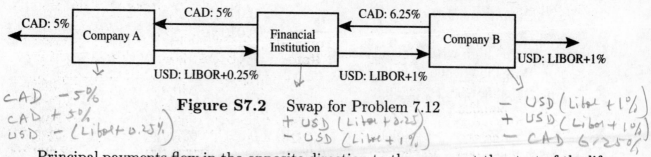

Figure S7.2 Swap for Problem 7.12

(handwriting under Company A): CAD −5% / CAD +5% / USD −(Libor+0.25%)

(handwriting under Financial Institution): + USD (Libor +0.25) / − USD (Libor +1%)

(handwriting under Company B): − USD (Libor +1%) / + USD (Libor +1%) / − CAD 6.25%

Principal payments flow in the opposite direction to the arrows at the start of the life of the swap and in the same direction as the arrows at the end of the life of the swap. The financial institution would be exposed to some foreign exchange risk which could be hedged using forward contracts.

(handwriting): + CAD 6.25% / − CAD 5%

45

(handwriting): Net +0.75 +1.25 / USD   CAD / = 1.50

Problem 7.13.

After it hedges its foreign exchange risk using forward contracts, is the financial institution's average spread in Figure 7.10 likely to be greater than or less than 20 basis points? Explain your answer.

The financial institution will have to buy 1.1% of the AUD principal in the forward market for each year of the life of the swap. Since AUD interest rates are higher than dollar interest rates, AUD is at a discount in forward markets. This means that the AUD purchased for year 2 is less expensive than that purchased for year 1; the AUD purchased for year 3 is less expensive than that purchased for year 2; and so on. This works in favor of the financial institution and means that its spread increases with time. The spread is always above 20 basis points.

Problem 7.14.

"Companies with high credit risks are the ones that cannot access fixed-rate markets directly. They are the companies that are most likely to be paying fixed and receiving floating in an interest rate swap." Assume that this statement is true. Do you think it increases or decreases the risk of a financial institution's swap portfolio? Assume that companies are most likely to default when interest rates are high.

Consider a plain-vanilla interest rate swap involving two companies X and Y. We suppose that X is paying fixed and receiving floating while Y is paying floating and receiving fixed.

The quote suggests that company X will usually be less creditworthy than company Y. (Company X might be a BBB-rated company that has difficulty in accessing fixed-rate markets directly; company Y might be a AAA-rated company that has no difficulty accessing fixed or floating rate markets.) Presumably company X wants fixed-rate funds and company Y wants floating-rate funds.

The financial institution will realize a loss if company Y defaults when rates are high or if company X defaults when rates are low. These events are relatively unlikely since (a) Y is unlikely to default in any circumstances and (b) defaults are less likely to happen when rates are low. For the purposes of illustration, suppose that the probabilities of various events are as follows:

Default by Y:	0.001
Default by X:	0.010
Rates high when default occurs:	0.7
Rates low when default occurs:	0.3

The probability of a loss is

$$0.001 \times 0.7 + 0.010 \times 0.3 = 0.0037$$

If the roles of X and Y in the swap had been reversed the probability of a loss would be

$$0.001 \times 0.3 + 0.010 \times 0.7 = 0.0073$$

Assuming companies are more likely to default when interest rates are high, the above argument shows that the observation in quotes has the effect of decreasing the risk of a financial institution's swap portfolio. It is worth noting that the assumption that defaults are more likely when interest rates are high is open to question. The assumption is motivated by the thought that high interest rates often lead to financial difficulties for corporations. However, there is often a time lag between interest rates being high and the resultant default. When the default actually happens interest rates may be relatively low.

Problem 7.15.

Why is the expected loss from a default on a swap less than the expected loss from the default on a loan with the same principal?

In an interest-rate swap a financial institution's exposure depends on the difference between a fixed-rate of interest and a floating-rate of interest. It has no exposure to the notional principal. In a loan the whole principal can be lost.

Problem 7.16.

A bank finds that its assets are not matched with its liabilities. It is taking floating-rate deposits and making fixed-rate loans. How can swaps be used to offset the risk?

The bank is paying a floating-rate on the deposits and receiving a fixed-rate on the loans. It can offset its risk by entering into interest rate swaps (with other financial institutions or corporations) in which it contracts to pay fixed and receive floating.

Problem 7.17.

Explain how you would value a swap that is the exchange of a floating rate in one currency for a fixed rate in another currency. see Problem 7.12

The floating payments can be valued in currency A by (i) assuming that the forward rates are realized, and (ii) discounting the resulting cash flows at appropriate currency A discount rates. Suppose that the value is V_A. The fixed payments can be valued in currency B by discounting them at the appropriate currency B discount rates. Suppose that the value is V_B. If Q is the current exchange rate (number of units of currency A per unit of currency B), the value of the swap in currency A is $V_A - QV_B$. Alternatively, it is $V_A/Q - V_B$ in currency B.

2yr   3yr $+\dfrac{5.4}{5.6}$
$\dfrac{11.0}{} \div 2 = 5.5\%$

Problem 7.18.

The LIBOR zero curve is flat at 5% (continuously compounded) out to 1.5 years. Swap rates for 2- and 3-year semiannual pay swaps are 5.4% and 5.6%, respectively. Estimate the LIBOR zero rates for maturities of 2.0, 2.5, and 3.0 years. (Assume that the 2.5-year swap rate is the average of the 2- and 3-year swap rates.)

The two-year swap rate is [given] 5.4%. This means that a two-year LIBOR bond paying a semiannual coupon at the rate of 5.4% per annum sells for par. If R_2 is the two-year LIBOR zero rate

2.63334   2.56832   2.50490   [Sum] 7.70656

$$2.7e^{-0.05 \times 0.5} + 2.7e^{-0.05 \times 1.0} + 2.7e^{-0.05 \times 1.5} + 102.7e^{-R_2 \times 2.0} = 100$$

.97531   .95123   .92774

$\dfrac{5.4}{2} = 2.7$

$102.7\, e^{-R_2 \cdot 2.0}$ ⁴⁷ $= 100 - 7.70656 = 92.29334$

$e^{-R_2 \cdot 2.0} = \dfrac{92.29334}{102.7} = .89867$ Take logs

$-2R_2 = \ln .89867 = -0.10684$

$R_2 = \dfrac{.10684}{2} = .05342$

Solving this gives $R_2 = 0.05342$. The 2.5-year swap rate is assumed to be 5.5%. This
means that a 2.5-year LIBOR bond paying a semiannual coupon at the rate of 5.5% per
annum sells for par. If $R_{2.5}$ is the 2.5-year LIBOR zero rate

[handwritten, margin left: 2.75 is half of 5.5%]
[handwritten above terms: 2.68210   2.61588   2.55429   2.47134]
[handwritten note above: average of 2 yr & 3 yr rate.]

$$2.75e^{-0.05\times0.5}+2.75e^{-0.05\times1.0}+2.75e^{-0.05\times1.5}+2.75e^{-0.05342\times2.0}+102.75e^{-R_{2.5}\times2.5}=100$$

[handwritten under terms: .97531   .95123   .92774   .89867 (given)]

Solving this gives $R_{2.5} = 0.05442$. The 3-year swap rate is 5.6%. This means that a 3-year
LIBOR bond paying a semiannual coupon at the rate of 5.6% per annum sells for par. If
R_3 is the three-year LIBOR zero rate

[handwritten above terms: 2.73087   2.66744   2.59767   2.51628   2.44384]

$$2.8e^{-0.05\times0.5}+2.8e^{-0.05\times1.0}+2.8e^{-0.05\times1.5}+2.8e^{-0.05342\times2.0}+2.8e^{-0.05442\times2.5}$$

[handwritten under terms: .97531   .95123   .92774   .89867   .87280]

$$+102.8e^{-R_3\times3.0}=100$$

Solving this gives $R_3 = 0.05544$. The zero rates for maturities 2.0, 2.5, and 3.0 years are
therefore 5.342%, 5.442%, and 5.544%, respectively.

[handwritten work:]

$$12.95210 + 102.8\,e^{-R_3\times3.0} = 100$$

$$102.8\,e^{-R_3\times3.0} = 100 - 12.95210$$

$$102.8\,e^{-R_3\cdot3.0} = 87.04790$$

$$e^{-R_3\cdot3.0} = \frac{87.04790}{102.8} = 0.84677$$

Take logs

$$-3R_3 = -0.16633$$

$$R_3 = 0.05544$$

[handwritten lower section:]

$$102.75\,e^{-R_{2.5}\times2.5} = 100 - 10.32061 = 89.67939 \div 102.75 = .87279$$

Take log of both sides

$$(-R_{2.5}\times2.5) = \ln 0.87279 = -0.13606$$

$$-R_{2.5} = \frac{-.13606}{2.5}$$

$$R_{2.5} = .05442$$

CHAPTER 8
Securitization and the Credit Crisis of 2007

This chapter covers issues arising from the credit crisis that started in 2007. It explains how securitization works, discusses what happened to the US real estate market during the first decade of the 21st century, and speculates on what is needed to avoid futures crises.

There are two securities you should understand: ABSs and ABS CDOs. There are two ways of describing how these securities work. One is in terms of the waterfall (see Figure 8.2): cash flows go first to the most senior tranche, then to the next-most-senior tranche, and so on. The other is in terms of who bears the losses: losses are borne first by the most junior tranche, then by the next-most-junior tranche, and so on. The ABS tranches we are concerned with are created from a portfolio of subprime mortgages. ABS CDO tranches are created from a portfolio of BBB-rated ABS tranches. Make sure you understand how Table 8.1 is calculated from Figure 8.3.

The subprime story in Section 8.2 is fairly simple. Lenders relaxed their criteria for granting mortgages. More people were able to borrow money to buy their first home. The demand for houses increased. House prices therefore increased. When people found they could not afford their mortgages, there were foreclosures. The supply of houses then exceeded the demand and prices decreased. This led to losses on the ABSs and ABS CDOs that were created from mortgages. Investors panicked and moved to safe securities such as Treasury bonds and credit spreads increased. Banks that had invested in the tranches of ABSs and ABS CDOs lost a lot of money.

Not surprisingly, it is taking some time to sort out the resulting mess. There have been many proposals to change the regulations that govern the way banks and other financial institutions operate. It is now realized that there were mistakes in the way the risks in tranches of ABS CDOs were assessed (see Section 8.3.) As explained in Section 8.4, there are moves afoot to regulate what happens when credit risks are transferred in the economy, to change the way bonuses are calculated, to increase transparency of the trades that are done, and to use models more effectively.

SOLUTIONS TO PRACTICE QUESTIONS

Problem 8.8.

Why did mortgage lenders frequently not check on information provided by potential borrowers on mortgage application forms during the 2000 to 2007 period?

Subprime mortgages were frequently securitized. The only information that was retained during the securitization process was the applicant's FICO score and the loan-to-value ratio of the mortgage.

Problem 8.9.

How were the risks in ABS CDOs misjudged by the market?

Investors underestimated how high the default correlations between mortgages would be in stressed market conditions. Investors also did not always realize that the tranches underlying ABS CDOs were usually quite thin so that they were either totally wiped out or untouched. There was an unfortunate tendency to assume that a tranche with a particular rating could be considered to be the same as a bond with that rating. This assumption is not valid for the reasons just mentioned.

Problem 8.10.

What is meant by the term "agency costs"? How did agency costs play a role in the credit crisis?

"Agency costs" is a term used to describe the costs in a situation where the interests of two parties are not perfectly aligned. There were potential agency costs between a) the originators of mortgages and investors and b) employees of banks who earned bonuses and the banks themselves.

Problem 8.11.

How is an ABS CDO created? What was the motivation to create ABS CDOs?

Typically an ABS CDO is created from the BBB-rated tranches of an ABS. This is because it is difficult to find investors in a direct way for the BBB-rated tranches of an ABS.

Problem 8.12.

Explain the impact of an increase in default correlation on the risks of the senior tranche of an ABS. What is its impact on the risks of the equity tranche?

As default correlation increases, the senior tranche of a CDO becomes more risky because it is more likely to suffer losses. As default correlation increases, the equity tranche becomes less risky. To understand why this is so, note that in the limit when there is perfect correlation there is a high probability that there will be no defaults and the equity tranche will suffer no losses.

Problem 8.13.

Explain why the AAA-rated tranche of an ABS CDO is more risky than the AAA-rated tranche of an ABS.

A moderately high default rate will wipe out the tranches underlying the ABS CDO so that the AAA-rated tranche of the ABS CDO is also wiped out. A moderately high default rate will at worst wipe out only part of the AAA-rated tranche of an ABS.

Problem 8.14.

Explain why the end-of-year bonus is sometimes referred to as "short-term compensation."

The end-of-year bonus usually reflects performance during the year. This types of compensation tends to lead traders and other employees of banks to focus on their next bonus and therefore have a short-term time horizon for their decision making.

CHAPTER 9
Mechanics of Options Markets

If you already understand how options work you will not have to spend a lot of time on Chapter 9. Bear in mind that, for every trader buying an option, there is another trader selling it. Make sure you understand the profit diagrams in Figures 9.1 to 9.4. Figure 9.5 shows the payoffs from the four different option strategies in Figures 9.1 to 9.4. Whereas the profit takes account of the initial amount paid for the option, the payoff does not.

Make sure you understand the terminology of option markets: American options, European options, strike price, expiration date, intrinsic value, option class, option series, in-the-money, at-the-money, out-of-the-money, flex options, option writing and so on.

Except in special circumstances (see Business Snapshot 9.1) there is no adjustment to the terms of an option for cash dividends. Stock dividends and stock splits do lead to adjustments. For example, a 3-for-1 stock split leads to the strike price being reduced to a third of what it was before and the number of options held being multiplied by 3. A 10% stock dividend is like a 1.1 for 1 stock split. It leads to the strike price being reduced to 10/11 of what it was before and the number of options held being increased by 10%.

Traders who sell (i.e., write) options must maintain margin accounts similar to the margin accounts for futures traders. Traders who buy options pay for the options up front and do not maintain margin accounts.

Warrants issued by a company on its own stock are different from regular call options in that exercise of the warrants leads to the company issuing more shares. (When a regular call option on a stock is exercised, the option writer buys shares of the stock in the market and delivers them to the option holder.) Employee stock options and convertible bonds are similar to warrants in this respect.

Options trade in the over-the-counter market as well as the exchange-trade market. Indeed for many types of underlyings (e.g., exchange rates and interest rates) the over-the-counter market is much bigger than the exchange-traded market. The options traded over the counter do not have to have the standard terms defined by exchanges. The terms can be chosen to meet the precise needs of corporate treasurers and fund managers. Sometimes the options have a different structure from regular options. They are then referred to as exotic options (or just exotics).

SOLUTIONS TO PRACTICE QUESTIONS

Problem 9.8.

A corporate treasurer is designing a hedging program involving foreign currency options. What are the pros and cons of using (a) the NASDAQ OMX and (b) the over-the-counter market for trading?

The NASDAQ OMX offers options with standard strike prices and times to maturity. Options in the over-the-counter market have the advantage that they can be tailored to meet the precise needs of the treasurer. Their disadvantage is that they expose the treasurer to some credit risk. Exchanges organize their trading so that there is virtually no credit risk.

Problem 9.9.

Suppose that a European call option to buy a share for $100.00 costs $5.00 and is held until maturity. Under what circumstances will the holder of the option make a profit? Under what circumstances will the option be exercised? Draw a diagram illustrating how the profit from a long position in the option depends on the stock price at maturity of the option.

Ignoring the time value of money, the holder of the option will make a profit if the stock price at maturity of the option is greater than $105. This is because the payoff to the holder of the option is, in these circumstances, greater than the $5 paid for the option. The option will be exercised if the stock price at maturity is greater than $100. Note that if the stock price is between $100 and $105 the option is exercised, but the holder of the option takes a loss overall. The profit from a long position is as shown in Figure S9.1.

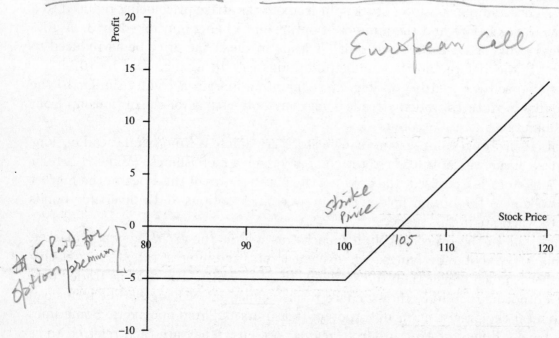

Figure S9.1   Profit from long position in Problem 9.9

Problem 9.10.

Suppose that a European put option to sell a share for $60 costs $8 and is held until maturity. Under what circumstances will the seller of the option (the party with the short position) make a profit? Under what circumstances will the option be exercised? Draw a diagram illustrating how the profit from a short position in the option depends on the stock price at maturity of the option.

Ignoring the time value of money, the seller of the option will make a profit if the stock price at maturity is greater than $52.00. This is because the cost to the seller of the

52

option is in these circumstances less than the price received for the option. The option will be exercised if the stock price at maturity is less than $60.00. Note that if the stock price is between $52.00 and $60.00 the seller of the option makes a profit even though the option is exercised. The profit from the short position is as shown in Figure S9.2.

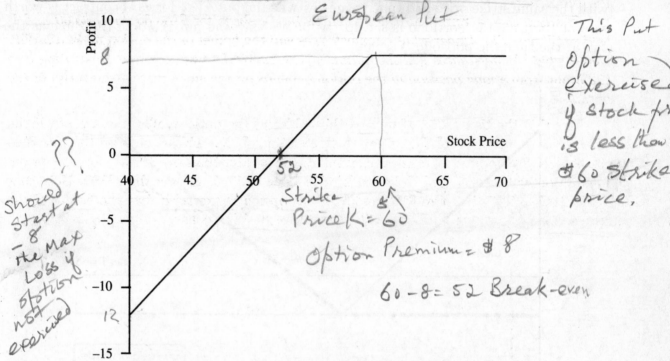

Handwritten annotations: European Put

This Put Option exercised if stock price is less than $60 strike price.

?? Should start at -8 the Max Loss if option not exercised

52 Strike Price K = 60

Option Premium = $8

60 - 8 = 52 Break-even

Figure S9.2 Profit from short position in Problem 9.10

Problem 9.11.

Describe the terminal value of the following portfolio: a newly entered-into long forward contract on an asset and a long position in a European put option on the asset with the same maturity as the forward contract and a strike price that is equal to the forward price of the asset at the time the portfolio is set up. Show that the European put option has the same value as a European call option with the same strike price and maturity.

The terminal value of the long forward contract is:

$$S_T - F_0$$

where S_T is the price of the asset at maturity and F_0 is the forward price of the asset at the time the portfolio is set up. (The delivery price in the forward contract is also F_0.)

The terminal value of the put option is:

$$\max(F_0 - S_T, 0)$$

The terminal value of the portfolio is therefore

$$S_T - F_0 + \max(F_0 - S_T, 0) = \max(0, S_T - F_0]$$

Handwritten: Check

1) $S_T > F_0$

2) $F_0 > S_T$

53

This is the same as the terminal value of a European call option with the same maturity as the forward contract and an exercise price equal to F_0. This result is illustrated in the Figure S9.3.

We have shown that the forward contract plus the put is worth the same as a call with the same strike price and time to maturity as the put. The forward contract is worth zero at the time the portfolio is set up. It follows that the put is worth the same as the call at the time the portfolio is set up.

check

Figure S9.3   Profit from portfolio in Problem 9.11

Problem 9.12.

A trader buys a call option with a strike price of $45 and a put option with a strike price of $40. Both options have the same maturity. The call costs $3 and the put costs $4. Draw a diagram showing the variation of the trader's profit with the asset price.

Figure S9.4 shows the variation of the trader's position with the asset price. We can divide the alternative asset prices into three ranges:

(a) When the asset price less than $40, the put option provides a payoff of $40 - S_T$ and the call option provides no payoff. The options cost $7 and so the total profit is $33 - S_T$.

(b) When the asset price is between $40 and $45, neither option provides a payoff. There is a net loss of $7.

(c) When the asset price greater than $45, the call option provides a payoff of $S_T - 45$ and the put option provides no payoff. Taking into account the $7 cost of the options, the total profit is $S_T - 52$.

The trader makes a profit (ignoring the time value of money) if the stock price is less than $33 or greater than $52. This type of trading strategy is known as a strangle and is discussed in Chapter 11.

Figure S9.4 Profit from trading strategy in Problem 9.12

Handwritten annotations on figure:
Call Premium = $3
Put Premium = $4
Put option
Payoff = 40 - ST
when asset price is less than 40
call has no payoff
Call
Call
Put
Total Profit = 33 - ST
Put strike Price
Call strike Price 45
Asset Price
Total Profit = ST - 52
#3 { Call Premium
} = $4 Put premium
Call
Put
Put
Profit if stock price is less than $33 or more than $52
Net Loss $7 Between ST at $40 to $45

Legend:
······ Call
—— Put
━━ Total

Problem 9.13.

Explain why an American option is always worth at least as much as a European option on the same asset with the same strike price and exercise date.

The holder of an American option has all the same rights as the holder of a European option and more. It must therefore be worth at least as much. If it were not, an arbitrageur could short the European option and take a long position in the American option.

Problem 9.14.

Explain why an American option is always worth at least as much as its intrinsic value.

The holder of an American option has the right to exercise it immediately. The American option must therefore be worth at least as much as its intrinsic value. If it were not an arbitrageur could lock in a sure profit by buying the option and exercising it immediately.

Problem 9.15.

Explain carefully the difference between writing a put option and buying a call option.

Writing a put gives a payoff of $\min(S_T - K, 0)$. Buying a call gives a payoff of $\max(S_T - K, 0)$. In both cases the potential payoff is $S_T - K$. The difference is that for a written put the counterparty chooses whether you get the payoff (and will allow you to get it only when it is negative to you). For a long call you decide whether you get the payoff (and you choose to get it when it is positive to you.)

Problem 9.16.

The treasurer of a corporation is trying to choose between options and forward contracts to hedge the corporation's foreign exchange risk. Discuss the advantages and disadvantages of each.

Forward contracts lock in the exchange rate that will apply to a particular transaction in the future. Options provide insurance that the exchange rate will not be worse than some level. The advantage of a forward contract is that uncertainty is eliminated as far as possible. The disadvantage is that the outcome with hedging can be significantly worse than the outcome with no hedging. This disadvantage is not as marked with options. However, unlike forward contracts, options involve an up-front cost.

Problem 9.17.

Consider an exchange-traded call option contract to buy 500 shares with a strike price of $40 and maturity in four months. Explain how the terms of the option contract change when there is

$K = 40$

    a. A 10% stock dividend
    b. A 10% cash dividend
    c. A 4-for-1 stock split

(a) The option contract becomes one to buy $500 \times 1.1 = 550$ shares with an exercise price $40/1.1 = 36.36$.

(b) There is no effect. The terms of an options contract are not normally adjusted for cash dividends.

(c) The option contract becomes one to buy $500 \times 4 = 2,000$ shares with an exercise price of $40/4 = \$10$.

Problem 9.18.

"If most of the call options on a stock are in the money, it is likely that the stock price has risen rapidly in the last few months." Discuss this statement.

The exchange has certain rules governing when trading in a new option is initiated. These mean that the option is close-to-the-money when it is first traded. If all call options are in the money it is therefore likely that the stock price has risen since trading in the option began.

Problem 9.19.

What is the effect of an unexpected cash dividend on (a) a call option price and (b) a put option price?

An unexpected cash dividend would reduce the stock price on the ex-dividend date. This stock price reduction would not be anticipated by option holders. As a result there would be a reduction in the value of a call option and an increase the value of a put option. (Note that the terms of an option are adjusted for cash dividends only in exceptional circumstances.)

skip out

Problem 9.20.

Options on General Motors stock are on a March, June, September, and December cycle. What options trade on (a) March 1, (b) June 30, and (c) August 5?

See Pg. 212. check

March 1 **(a)** March, April, June and September

June 30 **(b)** July, August, September, December

August 5 **(c)** August, September, December, March. Longer dated options may also trade.

Problem 9.21.

Explain why the market maker's bid-offer spread represents a real cost to options investors.

A "fair" price for the option can reasonably be assumed to be half way between the bid and the offer price quoted by a market maker. An investor typically buys at the market maker's offer and sells at the market maker's bid. Each time he or she does this there is a hidden cost equal to half the bid-offer spread.

Problem 9.22.

A United States investor writes five naked call option contracts. The option price is $3.50, the strike price is $60.00, and the stock price is $57.00. What is the initial margin requirement?

The two calculations are necessary to determine the initial margin. The first gives

Option Price · S_0 · Amt by which option is out of money

$$500 \times (3.5 + 0.2 \times 57 - 3) = 5,950$$

Sale Proceeds · 20% share price

The second gives

Sale Proceeds · Option Price · S_0

See Pg. 217

$$500 \times (3.5 + 0.1 \times 57) = 4,600$$

Sale Proceeds · 10% of Share Price

The initial margin is the greater of these, or $5,950. Part of this can be provided by the initial amount of $500 \times 3.5 = \$1,750$ received for the options.

CHAPTER 10
Properties of Stock Options

This chapter starts by considering the general way in which an option price depends on the stock price, strike price, time to expiration, volatility, risk-free rate, and dividends. Make sure you understand Table 10.1. An important point that often causes confusion is that Table 10.1 considers the change in a variable with all the other variables remaining the same. (This the usual assumption in calculus when partial derivatives are calculated.) For example, when considering interest rates it is assumed that interest rates change without any other variables changing. In practice when interest rates increase (decrease) stock prices tend to decrease (increase).

The rest of the chapter considers what we can say about option prices without making any assumptions about volatility or the way in which the stock price behaves. The arguments used are no arbitrage arguments. Section 10.3, for example, derives upper and lower bounds for call and put options. If the price of an option is outside the range given by the upper and lower bound there is a clear arbitrage opportunity. For example, if a call option is below the lower bound an arbitrageur buys the option and shorts the stock; if it is above the upper bound the arbitrageur buys the stock and sells the option.

Put-call parity (see equations 10.6 and 10.10) is a very important result. It shows that there is a relationship between the price of a European call option with a certain strike price and time to maturity and the price of a European put option with the same strike price and time to maturity. As illustrated in Table 10.3 there is an arbitrage opportunity if put–call parity does not hold. For American options put-call parity does not hold, but an inequality relationship can be derived (see equations 10.7 and 10.11).

An American call option on a stock that will not pay dividends during the life of the option should never be exercised early. This is because a) delaying exercise has the advantage that it delays paying the strike price and b) exercising early would give up the protection that the option holder has against the possibility of the stock price falling below the strike price by the end of the life of the option. American put options on stocks that do not pay a dividend are liable to be exercised early. Indeed, it can be shown that at any give time there is always a critical stock price below which it is optimal for the holder of the put option to exercise.

SOLUTIONS TO PRACTICE QUESTIONS

Problem 10.8.

Explain why the arguments leading to put–call parity for European options cannot be used to give a similar result for American options.

When early exercise is not possible, we can argue that two portfolios that are worth the same at time T must be worth the same at earlier times. When early exercise is possible, the argument falls down. Suppose that $P + S > C + Ke^{-rT}$. This situation does not lead to an arbitrage opportunity. If we buy the call, short the put, and short the stock, we cannot be sure of the result because we do not know when the put will be exercised.

Problem 10.9.

What is a lower bound for the price of a six-month call option on a non-dividend-paying stock when the stock price is $80, the strike price is $75, and the risk-free interest rate is 10% per annum?

The lower bound is

$$80 - 75e^{-0.1 \times 0.5} = \$8.66$$

Problem 10.10

What is a lower bound for the price of a two-month European put option on a non-dividend-paying stock when the stock price is $58, the strike price is $65, and the risk-free interest rate is 5% per annum?

The lower bound is

$$65e^{-0.05 \times 2/12} - 58 = \$6.46$$

Problem 10.11.

A four-month European call option on a dividend-paying stock is currently selling for $5. The stock price is $64, the strike price is $60, and a dividend of $0.80 is expected in one month. The risk-free interest rate is 12% per annum for all maturities. What opportunities are there for an arbitrageur?

The present value of the strike price is $60e^{-0.12 \times 4/12} = \$57.65$. The present value of the dividend is $0.80e^{-0.12 \times 1/12} = 0.79$. Because

$$5 < 64 - 57.65 - 0.79$$

the condition in equation (10.8) is violated. An arbitrageur should buy the option and short the stock. This generates $64 - 5 = \$59$. The arbitrageur invests $0.79 of this at 12% for one month to pay the dividend of $0.80 in one month. The remaining $58.21 is invested for four months at 12%. Regardless of what happens a profit will materialize.

If the stock price declines below $60 in four months, the arbitrageur loses the $5 spent on the option but gains on the short position. The arbitrageur shorts when the stock price is $64, has to pay dividends with a present value of $0.79, and closes out the short position when the stock price is $60 or less. Because $57.65 is the present value of $60, the short position generates at least $64 - 57.65 - 0.79 = \$5.56$ in present value terms. The present value of the arbitrageur's gain is therefore at least $5.56 - 5.00 = \$0.56$.

If the stock price is above $60 at the expiration of the option, the option is exercised. The arbitrageur buys the stock for $60 in four months and closes out the short position. The present value of the $60 paid for the stock is $57.65 and as before the dividend has a present value of $0.79. The gain from the short position and the exercise of the option is therefore exactly $64 - 57.65 - 0.79 = \$5.56$. The arbitrageur's gain in present value terms is exactly $5.56 - 5.00 = \$0.56$.

Problem 10.12.

A one-month European put option on a non-dividend-paying stock is currently selling for $2.50. The stock price is $47, the strike price is $50, and the risk-free interest rate is 6% per annum. What opportunities are there for an arbitrageur?

In this case the present value of the strike price is $50e^{-0.06 \times 1/12} = 49.75$. Because

$$2.5 < 49.75 - 47.00$$

the condition in equation (10.5) is violated. An arbitrageur should borrow $49.50 at 6% for one month, buy the stock, and buy the put option. This generates a profit in all circumstances.

If the stock price is above $50 in one month, the option expires worthless, but the stock can be sold for at least $50. A sum of $50 received in one month has a present value of $49.75 today. The strategy therefore generates profit with a present value of at least $0.25.

If the stock price is below $50 in one month the put option is exercised and the stock owned is sold for exactly $50 (or $49.75 in present value terms). The trading strategy therefore generates a profit of exactly $0.25 in present value terms.

Problem 10.13.

Give an intuitive explanation of why the early exercise of an American put becomes more attractive as the risk-free rate increases and volatility decreases.

The early exercise of an American put is attractive when the interest earned on the strike price is greater than the insurance element lost. When interest rates increase, the value of the interest earned on the strike price increases making early exercise more attractive. When volatility decreases, the insurance element is less valuable. Again this makes early exercise more attractive.

Problem 10.14.

The price of a European call that expires in six months and has a strike price of $30 is $2. The underlying stock price is $29, and a dividend of $0.50 is expected in two months and again in five months. The term structure is flat, with all risk-free interest rates being 10%. What is the price of a European put option that expires in six months and has a strike price of $30?

Using the notation in the chapter, put-call parity [equation (10.10)] gives

$$c + Ke^{-rT} + D = p + S_0$$

or

$$p = c + Ke^{-rT} + D - S_0$$

In this case

$$p = 2 + 30e^{-0.1 \times 6/12} + (0.5e^{-0.1 \times 2/12} + 0.5e^{-0.1 \times 5/12}) - 29 = 2.51$$

In other words the put price is $2.51.

Problem 10.15.

Explain carefully the arbitrage opportunities in Problem 10.14 if the European put price is $3.

If the put price is $3.00, it is too high relative to the call price. An arbitrageur should buy the call, short the put and short the stock. This generates $-2 + 3 + 29 = \$30$ in cash which is invested at 10%. Regardless of what happens a profit with a present value of $3.00 - 2.51 = \$0.49$ is locked in.

If the stock price is above $30 in six months, the call option is exercised, and the put option expires worthless. The call option enables the stock to be bought for $30, or $30e^{-0.10 \times 6/12} = \$28.54$ in present value terms. The dividends on the short position cost $0.5e^{-0.1 \times 2/12} + 0.5e^{-0.1 \times 5/12} = \$0.97$ in present value terms so that there is a profit with a present value of $30 - 28.54 - 0.97 = \$0.49$.

If the stock price is below $30 in six months, the put option is exercised and the call option expires worthless. The short put option leads to the stock being bought for $30, or $30e^{-0.10 \times 6/12} = \$28.54$ in present value terms. The dividends on the short position cost $0.5e^{-0.1 \times 2/12} + 0.5e^{-0.1 \times 5/12} = \$0.97$ in present value terms so that there is a profit with a present value of $30 - 28.54 - 0.97 = \$0.49$.

Problem 10.16.

The price of an American call on a non-dividend-paying stock is $4. The stock price is $31, the strike price is $30, and the expiration date is in three months. The risk-free interest rate is 8%. Derive upper and lower bounds for the price of an American put on the same stock with the same strike price and expiration date.

From equation (10.7)

$$S_0 - K \leq C - P \leq S_0 - Ke^{-rT}$$

In this case

$$31 - 30 \leq 4 - P \leq 31 - 30e^{-0.08 \times 0.25}$$

or

$$1.00 \leq 4.00 - P \leq 1.59$$

subtract 4 and change sign

or

$$2.41 \leq P \leq 3.00$$

Upper and lower bounds for the price of an American put are therefore $2.41 and $3.00.

Problem 10.17.

Explain carefully the arbitrage opportunities in Problem 10.16 if the American put price is greater than the calculated upper bound.

If the American put price is greater than $3.00 an arbitrageur can sell the American put, short the stock, and buy the American call. This realizes at least $3 + 31 - 4 = \$30$

which can be invested at the risk-free interest rate. At some stage during the 3-month period either the American put or the American call will be exercised. The arbitrageur then pays \$30, receives the stock and closes out the short position. The cash flows to the arbitrageur are +\$30 at time zero and −\$30 at some future time. These cash flows have a positive present value.

Problem 10.18.

Prove the result in equation (10.7). (Hint: For the first part of the relationship consider (a) a portfolio consisting of a European call plus an amount of cash equal to K and (b) a portfolio consisting of an American put option plus one share.)

As in the text we use c and p to denote the European call and put option price, and C and P to denote the American call and put option prices. Because $P \geq p$, it follows from put–call parity that

$$P \geq c + Ke^{-rT} - S_0$$

and since $c = C$,

$$P \geq C + Ke^{-rT} - S_0$$

or

$$C - P \leq S_0 - Ke^{-rT}$$

For a further relationship between C and P, consider

Portfolio I: One European call option plus an amount of cash equal to K.
Portfolio J: One American put option plus one share.

Both options have the same exercise price and expiration date. Assume that the cash in portfolio I is invested at the risk-free interest rate. If the put option is not exercised early portfolio J is worth

$$\max(S_T, K)$$

at time T. Portfolio I is worth

$$\max(S_T - K, 0) + Ke^{rT} = \max(S_T, K) - K + Ke^{rT}$$

at this time. Portfolio I is therefore worth more than portfolio J. Suppose next that the put option in portfolio J is exercised early, say, at time τ. This means that portfolio J is worth K at time τ. However, even if the call option were worthless, portfolio I would be worth $Ke^{r\tau}$ at time τ. It follows that portfolio I is worth at least as much as portfolio J in all circumstances. Hence

$$c + K \geq P + S_0$$

Since $c = C$,

$$C + K \geq P + S_0$$

or

$$C - P \geq S_0 - K$$

Combining this with the other inequality derived above for $C - P$, we obtain

$$S_0 - K \leq C - P \leq S_0 - Ke^{-rT}$$

Problem 10.19.

Prove the result in equation (10.11). (Hint: For the first part of the relationship consider (a) a portfolio consisting of a European call plus an amount of cash equal to $D + K$ and (b) a portfolio consisting of an American put option plus one share.)

As in the text we use c and p to denote the European call and put option price, and C and P to denote the American call and put option prices. The present value of the dividends will be denoted by D. As shown in the answer to Problem 10.18, when there are no dividends

$$C - P \le S_0 - Ke^{-rT}$$

Dividends reduce C and increase P. Hence this relationship must also be true when there are dividends.

For a further relationship between C and P, consider
    Portfolio I: one European call option plus an amount of cash equal to $D + K$
    Portfolio J: one American put option plus one share
Both options have the same exercise price and expiration date. Assume that the cash in portfolio I is invested at the risk-free interest rate. If the put option is not exercised early, portfolio J is worth

$$\max(S_T, K) + De^{rT}$$

at time T. Portfolio I is worth

$$\max(S_T - K, 0) + (D + K)e^{rT} = \max(S_T, K) + De^{rT} + Ke^{rT} - K$$

at this time. Portfolio I is therefore worth more than portfolio J. Suppose next that the put option in portfolio J is exercised early, say, at time τ. This means that portfolio J is worth at most $K + De^{r\tau}$ at time τ. However, even if the call option were worthless, portfolio I would be worth $(D + K)e^{r\tau}$ at time τ. It follows that portfolio I is worth more than portfolio J in all circumstances. Hence

$$c + D + K \ge P + S_0$$

Because $C \ge c$

$$C - P \ge S_0 - D - K$$

Problem 10.20.

Consider a five-year call option on a non-dividend-paying stock granted to employees. The option can be exercised at any time after the end off the first year. Unlike a regular exchange-traded call option, the employee stock option cannot be sold. What is the likely impact of this restriction on early exercise?

An employee stock option may be exercised early because the employee needs cash or because he or she is uncertain about the company's future prospects. Regular call options can be sold in the market in either of these two situations, but employee stock options cannot be sold. In theory an employee can short the company's stock as an alternative to

63

exercising. In practice this is not usually encouraged and may even be illegal for senior managers.

Problem 10.21.

Use the software DerivaGem to verify that Figures 10.1 and 10.2 are correct.

The graphs can be produced from the first worksheet in DerivaGem. Select Equity as the Underlying Type. Select Analytic European as the Option Type. Input stock price as 50, volatility as 30%, risk-free rate as 5%, time to exercise as 1 year, and exercise price as 50. Leave the dividend table blank because we are assuming no dividends. Select the button corresponding to call. Do not select the implied volatility button. Hit the *Enter* key and click on calculate. DerivaGem will show the price of the option as 7.15562248. Move to the Graph Results on the right hand side of the worksheet. Enter Option Price for the vertical axis and Asset price for the horizontal axis. Choose the minimum strike price value as 10 (software will not accept 0) and the maximum strike price value as 100. Hit *Enter* and click on *Draw Graph*. This will produce Figure 10.1a. Figures 10.1c, 10.1e, 10.2a, and 10.2c can be produced similarly by changing the horizontal axis. By selecting put instead of call and recalculating the rest of the figures can be produced. You are encouraged to experiment with this worksheet. Try different parameter values and different types of options.

CHAPTER 11
Trading Strategies Involving Options

This is a fun chapter that should not cause you too many problems. It describes some of the ways options can be used to produce interesting profit patterns. Figure 11.1 shows what can be achieved by taking a position in the option and the underlying asset. As put–call parity shows, a long or short position in the underlying asset can be used to convert a) a short put to something that looks like a short call, b) a long call to something that looks like a long put, c) a long put to something that looks like a long call, and d) a short put to something that looks like a short call.

Spread is the word used to describe a position in two or more calls or two or more puts. Put–call parity shows that a spread created using calls can also be created using puts. This is shown for four types of spreads in the chapter: bull spreads (see Figures 11.2 and 11.3); bear spreads (see Figures 11.4 and 11.5); butterfly spreads (see Figures 11.6 and 11.7); and calendar spreads (see Figures 11.8 and 11.9).

Combination is the word used to describe a position involving both calls and puts. A straddle involves buying a call and an put with the same strike price and maturity date. A strangle involves buying a call and a put when the strike price of the call is greater than that of the put.

In theory any payoff pattern can be created by using calls and puts with different strike prices in an appropriate way. Figure 11.13 shows that a butterfly spread can be used to create a payoff pattern that is a small "spike". Any specified payoff pattern can be by combining spikes judiciously.

SOLUTIONS TO PRACTICE QUESTIONS   *Do up to 11.16*

Problem 11.8.

Use put–call parity to relate the initial investment for a bull spread created using calls to the initial investment for a bull spread created using puts.

A bull spread using calls provides a profit pattern with the same general shape as a bull spread using puts (see Figures 11.2 and 11.3 in the text). Define p_1 and c_1 as the prices of put and call with strike price K_1 and p_2 and c_2 as the prices of a put and call with strike price K_2. From put-call parity

$$p_1 + S = c_1 + K_1 e^{-rT}$$

$$p_2 + S = c_2 + K_2 e^{-rT}$$

Hence:

$$p_1 - p_2 = c_1 - c_2 - (K_2 - K_1)e^{-rT}$$

This shows that the initial investment when the spread is created from puts is less than the initial investment when it is created from calls by an amount $(K_2 - K_1)e^{-rT}$. In fact as mentioned in the text the initial investment when the bull spread is created from puts is negative, while the initial investment when it is created from calls is positive.

The profit when calls are used to create the bull spread is higher than when puts are used by $(K_2 - K_1)(1 - e^{-rT})$. This reflects the fact that the call strategy involves an additional risk-free investment of $(K_2 - K_1)e^{-rT}$ over the put strategy. This earns interest of $(K_2 - K_1)e^{-rT}(e^{rT} - 1) = (K_2 - K_1)(1 - e^{-rT})$.

Problem 11.9.

Explain how an aggressive bear spread can be created using put options.

An aggressive bull spread using call options is discussed in the text. Both of the options used have relatively high strike prices. Similarly, an aggressive bear spread can be created using put options. Both of the options should be out of the money (that is, they should have relatively low strike prices). The spread then costs very little to set up because both of the puts are worth close to zero. In most circumstances the spread will provide zero payoff. However, there is a small chance that the stock price will fall fast so that on expiration both options will be in the money. The spread then provides a payoff equal to the difference between the two strike prices, $K_2 - K_1$.

Problem 11.10.

Suppose that put options on a stock with strike prices $30 and $35 cost $4 and $7, respectively. How can the options be used to create (a) a bull spread and (b) a bear spread? Construct a table that shows the profit and payoff for both spreads.

A bull spread is created by buying the $30 put and selling the $35 put. This strategy gives rise to an initial cash inflow of $3. The outcome is as follows:

Stock Price	Payoff	Profit
$S_T \geq 35$	0	3
$30 \leq S_T < 35$	$S_T - 35$	$S_T - 32$
$S_T < 30$	-5	-2

A bear spread is created by selling the $30 put and buying the $35 put. This strategy costs $3 initially. The outcome is as follows:

Stock Price	Payoff	Profit
$S_T \geq 35$	0	-3
$30 \leq S_T < 35$	$35 - S_T$	$32 - S_T$
$S_T < 30$	5	2

66

Problem 11.11.

Use put–call parity to show that the cost of a butterfly spread created from European puts is identical to the cost of a butterfly spread created from European calls.

Define c_1, c_2, and c_3 as the prices of calls with strike prices K_1, K_2 and K_3. Define p_1, p_2 and p_3 as the prices of puts with strike prices K_1, K_2 and K_3. With the usual notation

$$c_1 + K_1 e^{-rT} = p_1 + S$$

$$c_2 + K_2 e^{-rT} = p_2 + S$$

$$c_3 + K_3 e^{-rT} = p_3 + S$$

Hence

$$c_1 + c_3 - 2c_2 + (K_1 + K_3 - 2K_2)e^{-rT} = p_1 + p_3 - 2p_2$$

Because $K_2 - K_1 = K_3 - K_2$, it follows that $K_1 + K_3 - 2K_2 = 0$ and

$$c_1 + c_3 - 2c_2 = p_1 + p_3 - 2p_2$$

The cost of a butterfly spread created using European calls is therefore exactly the same as the cost of a butterfly spread created using European puts.

Problem 11.12.

A call with a strike price of \$60 costs \$6. A put with the same strike price and expiration date costs \$4. Construct a table that shows the profit from a straddle. For what range of stock prices would the straddle lead to a loss?

A straddle is created by buying both the call and the put. This strategy costs \$10. The profit/loss is shown in the following table:

Stock Price	Payoff	Profit
$S_T > 60$	$S_T - 60$	$S_T - 70$
$S_T \leq 60$	$60 - S_T$	$50 - S_T$

This shows that the straddle will lead to a loss if the final stock price is between \$50 and \$70.

Problem 11.13.

Construct a table showing the payoff from a bull spread when puts with strike prices K_1 and K_2 are used ($K_2 > K_1$).

The bull spread is created by buying a put with strike price K_1 and selling a put with strike price K_2. The payoff is calculated as follows:

Stock Price Range	Payoff from Long Put Option	Payoff from Short Put Option	Total Payoff
$S_T \geq K_2$	0	0	0
$K_1 < S_T < K_2$	0	$S_T - K_2$	$-(K_2 - S_T)$
$S_T \leq K_1$	$K_1 - S_T$	$S_T - K_2$	$-(K_2 - K_1)$

Problem 11.14.

An investor believes that there will be a big jump in a stock price, but is uncertain as to the direction. Identify six different strategies the investor can follow and explain the differences among them.

Possible strategies are:

Strangle
Straddle
Strip
Strap
Reverse calendar spread
Reverse butterfly spread

The strategies all provide positive profits when there are large stock price moves. A strangle is less expensive than a straddle, but requires a bigger move in the stock price in order to provide a positive profit. Strips and straps are more expensive than straddles but provide bigger profits in certain circumstances. A strip will provide a bigger profit when there is a large downward stock price move. A strap will provide a bigger profit when there is a large upward stock price move. In the case of strangles, straddles, strips and straps, the profit increases as the size of the stock price movement increases. By contrast in a reverse calendar spread and a reverse butterfly spread there is a maximum potential profit regardless of the size of the stock price movement.

Problem 11.15.

How can a forward contract on a stock with a particular delivery price and delivery date be created from options?

Suppose that the delivery price is K and the delivery date is T. The forward contract is created by buying a European call and selling a European put when both options have strike price K and exercise date T. This portfolio provides a payoff of $S_T - K$ under all circumstances where S_T is the stock price at time T. Suppose that F_0 is the forward price. If $K = F_0$, the forward contract that is created has zero value. This shows that the price of a call equals the price of a put when the strike price is F_0.

Problem 11.16.

"A box spread comprises four options. Two can be combined to create a long forward position and two can be combined to create a short forward position." Explain this statement.

A box spread is a bull spread created using calls and a bear spread created using puts. With the notation in the text it consists of a) a long call with strike K_1, b) a short call with strike K_2, c) a long put with strike K_2, and d) a short put with strike K_1. a) and d) give a long forward contract with delivery price K_1; b) and c) give a short forward contract with delivery price K_2. The two forward contracts taken together give the payoff of $K_2 - K_1$.

Do up to here.

Problem 11.17.

What is the result if the strike price of the put is higher than the strike price of the call in a strangle?

The result is shown in Figure S11.1. The profit pattern from a long position in a call and a put when the put has a higher strike price than a call is much the same as when the call has a higher strike price than the put. Both the initial investment and the final payoff are much higher in the first case

Figure S11.1   Profit Pattern in Problem 11.17

Problem 11.18.

One Australian dollar is currently worth $0.64. A one-year butterfly spread is set up using European call options with strike prices of $0.60, $0.65, and $0.70. The risk-free interest rates in the United States and Australia are 5% and 4% respectively, and the *volatility of the exchange rate is 15%. Use the DerivaGem software to calculate the cost of setting up the butterfly spread position. Show that the cost is the same if European put options are used instead of European call options.*

To use DerivaGem select the first worksheet and choose Currency as the Underlying Type. Select Analytic European as the Option Type. Input exchange rate as 0.64, volatility as 15%, risk-free rate as 5%, foreign risk-free interest rate as 4%, time to exercise as 1 year, and exercise price as 0.60. Select the button corresponding to call. Do not select the implied volatility button. Hit the *Enter* key and click on calculate. DerivaGem will show the price of the option as 0.0618. Change the exercise price to 0.65, hit *Enter*, and click on calculate again. DerivaGem will show the value of the option as 0.0352. Change the exercise price to 0.70, hit *Enter*, and click on calculate. DerivaGem will show the value of the option as 0.0181.

Now select the button corresponding to put and repeat the procedure. DerivaGem shows the values of puts with strike prices 0.60, 0.65, and 0.70 to be 0.0176, 0.0386, and 0.0690, respectively.

The cost of setting up the butterfly spread when calls are used is therefore

$$0.0618 + 0.0181 - 2 \times 0.0352 = 0.0095$$

The cost of setting up the butterfly spread when puts are used is

$$0.0176 + 0.0690 - 2 \times 0.0386 = 0.0094$$

Allowing for rounding errors these two are the same.

CHAPTER 12
Introduction to Binomial Trees

This chapter introduces binomial trees. There are a number of reasons why binomial trees are covered at this relatively early stage in the book:

1. Binomial trees illustrate the no-arbitrage arguments that can be used to derive the Black–Scholes model (Chapter 13)
2. Binomial trees illustrate the delta hedging strategies that can be used to hedge a position in an option with a position in the underlying asset (Chapter 17)
3. Binomial trees illustrate the risk-neutral valuation argument. This is of central importance in derivatives' pricing
4. Binomial trees constitute an important numerical procedure for valuing American options. (Chapter 18.)

The chapter starts by considering one-step binomial trees for call options on a stock (see, for example, Figure 12.1). The option lasts until time T and there are assumed to be only two possible stock prices at time T and therefore and only two possible option prices. We consider portfolios consisting of a short position in one call option and a long position in Δ (delta) shares of the stock. For some value of Δ the portfolio has the same value for both of the possible final stock prices. We determine this value of Δ (see equation 12.1). For this value of Δ the portfolio is riskless because its payoff at time T is known for certain. As such it must earn the risk-free rate. The value of the portfolio today is the present value of the portfolio at time T. The value of the stock price is known today. The value of the option price can therefore be calculated. (See equations 12.2 and 12.3.)

Section 12.2 shows that in the case of a one-step binomial tree the option can be valued by

1. Assuming that the expected return on the stock is the risk-free rate; and
2. Discounting the expected payoff on the option at the risk-free rate.

This is the risk-neutral valuation argument. It is a very important argument in option pricing. It says that if we assume that all market participants are risk-neutral (in the sense that they require the risk-free rate as the expected return on all risky assets) then we get the right price for options. The price is not just correct in a risk-neutral world. It is correct in all other worlds as well.

Section 12.3 covers two-step binomial trees. In these the life of the option is divided into two equal time steps. The change in the stock price during each time step is assumed to be given by a one-step binomial tree (with the proportional up- and down-movements being the same.) This means that there are three possible final stock prices. (See for example Figure 12.3.) Evaluating the price of the option involves working back through the tree applying the risk-neutral analysis given in Section 12.2. The procedure for evaluating a put option is analogous to the procedure for valuing a call option. If the option is American we test whether early exercise is optimal at each node of the tree by calculating the value of the option with and without early exercise and taking the greater of the two. You should compare Figures 12.7 and 12.8 and make sure you understand the difference. They are being used to value the same option except that in Figure 12.7 the option is European whereas in Figure 12.8 it is American.

Once you have mastered two-step trees it is not difficult to extend the ideas in the chapter to multistep trees. Section 12.7 gives formulas for calculating the proportional up movement, u, the proportional down movement, d, and the risk-neutral probability of an up movement, p, from the stock price volatility, σ, the length of the time step, Δt, and the risk-free rate, r. The formulas are:

$$u = e^{\sigma \sqrt{\Delta t}}$$

$$d = \frac{1}{u}$$

$$p = \frac{a - d}{u - d}$$

where

$$a = e^{r \Delta t}$$

The last part of the chapter looks ahead to later chapters and explains how the binomial tree methodology can be used to value call and put options on stock indices, currencies, and futures contracts. The formulas are the same as those given above except that

$$a = e^{(r-q)\Delta t}$$

where
1. In the case of an option on a stock index, q is the average dividend yield on the index during the life of the option
2. In the case of an option on a foreign currency, q is the foreign risk-free rate
3. In the case of an option on a futures contract, $q = r$ so that $a = 1$

You are strongly recommended to use the DerivaGem software and inspect the binomial trees it produces. A step by step procedure for using the software is at the end of Section 12.8. Examples 12.1, 12.2, and 12.3 in Section 12.9 show DerivaGem output.

SOLUTIONS TO PRACTICE QUESTIONS

Problem 12.8.
Consider the situation in which stock price movements during the life of a European option are governed by a two-step binomial tree. Explain why it is not possible to set up a position in the stock and the option that remains riskless for the whole of the life of the option.

The riskless portfolio consists of a short position in the option and a long position in Δ shares. Because Δ changes during the life of the option, this riskless portfolio must also change.

Problem 12.9.

A stock price is currently $50. It is known that at the end of two months it will be either $53 or $48. The risk-free interest rate is 10% per annum with continuous compounding. What is the value of a two-month European call option with a strike price of $49? Use no-arbitrage arguments.

At the end of two months the value of the option will be either $4 (if the stock price is $53) or $0 (if the stock price is $48). Consider a portfolio consisting of:

$$+\Delta \quad : \quad \text{shares}$$
$$-1 \quad : \quad \text{option}$$

The value of the portfolio is either 48Δ or $53\Delta - 4$ in two months. If

$$48\Delta = 53\Delta - 4$$

i.e.,

$$\Delta = 0.8$$

the value of the portfolio is certain to be 38.4. For this value of Δ the portfolio is therefore riskless. The current value of the portfolio is:

$$0.8 \times 50 - f$$

where f is the value of the option. Since the portfolio must earn the risk-free rate of interest

$$(0.8 \times 50 - f)e^{0.10 \times 2/12} = 38.4$$

i.e.,

$$f = 2.23$$

The value of the option is therefore $2.23.

This can also be calculated directly from equations (12.2) and (12.3). $u = 1.06$, $d = 0.96$ so that

$$p = \frac{e^{0.10 \times 2/12} - 0.96}{1.06 - 0.96} = 0.5681$$

and

$$f = e^{-0.10 \times 2/12} \times 0.5681 \times 4 = 2.23$$

Problem 12.10.

A stock price is currently $80. It is known that at the end of four months it will be either $75 or $85. The risk-free interest rate is 5% per annum with continuous compounding. What is the value of a four-month European put option with a strike price of $80? Use no-arbitrage arguments.

At the end of four months the value of the option will be either $5 (if the stock price is $75) or $0 (if the stock price is $85). Consider a portfolio consisting of:

$$-\Delta \quad : \quad \text{shares}$$
$$+1 \quad : \quad \text{option}$$

73

(Note: The delta, Δ of a put option is negative. We have constructed the portfolio so that it is $+1$ option and $-\Delta$ shares rather than -1 option and $+\Delta$ shares so that the initial investment is positive.)

The value of the portfolio is either -85Δ or $-75\Delta + 5$ in four months. If

$$-85\Delta = -75\Delta + 5$$

i.e.,

$$\Delta = -0.5$$

the value of the portfolio is certain to be 42.5. For this value of Δ the portfolio is therefore riskless. The current value of the portfolio is:

$$0.5 \times 80 + f$$

where f is the value of the option. Since the portfolio is riskless

$$(0.5 \times 80 + f)e^{0.05 \times 4/12} = 42.5$$

i.e.,

$$f = 1.80$$

The value of the option is therefore $1.80.

This can also be calculated directly from equations (12.2) and (12.3). $u = 1.0625$, $d = 0.9375$ so that

$$p = \frac{e^{0.05 \times 4/12} - 0.9375}{1.0625 - 0.9375} = 0.6345$$

$1 - p = 0.3655$ and

$$f = e^{-0.05 \times 4/12} \times 0.3655 \times 5 = 1.80$$

Problem 12.11.

A stock price is currently $40. It is known that at the end of three months it will be either $45 or $35. The risk-free rate of interest with quarterly compounding is 8% per annum. Calculate the value of a three-month European put option on the stock with an exercise price of $40. Verify that no-arbitrage arguments and risk-neutral valuation arguments give the same answers.

At the end of three months the value of the option is either $5 (if the stock price is $35) or $0 (if the stock price is $45).

Consider a portfolio consisting of:

$$-\Delta \; : \; \text{shares}$$
$$+1 \; : \; \text{option}$$

(Note: The delta, Δ, of a put option is negative. We have constructed the portfolio so that it is $+1$ option and $-\Delta$ shares rather than -1 option and $+\Delta$ shares so that the initial investment is positive.)

The value of the portfolio is either $-35\Delta + 5$ or -45Δ. If:

$$-35\Delta + 5 = -45\Delta$$

i.e.,

$$\Delta = -0.5$$

the value of the portfolio is certain to be 22.5. For this value of Δ the portfolio is therefore riskless. The current value of the portfolio is

$$-40\Delta + f$$

where f is the value of the option. Since the portfolio must earn the risk-free rate of interest

$$(40 \times 0.5 + f) \times 1.02 = 22.5$$

Hence

$$f = 2.06$$

i.e., the value of the option is \$2.06.

This can also be calculated using risk-neutral valuation. Suppose that p is the probability of an upward stock price movement in a risk-neutral world. We must have

$$45p + 35(1 - p) = 40 \times 1.02$$

i.e.,

$$10p = 5.8$$

or:

$$p = 0.58$$

The expected value of the option in a risk-neutral world is:

$$0 \times 0.58 + 5 \times 0.42 = 2.10$$

This has a present value of

$$\frac{2.10}{1.02} = 2.06$$

This is consistent with the no-arbitrage answer.

Problem 12.12.

A stock price is currently \$50. Over each of the next two three-month periods it is expected to go up by 6% or down by 5%. The risk-free interest rate is 5% per annum with continuous compounding. What is the value of a six-month European call option with a strike price of \$51?

A tree describing the behavior of the stock price is shown in Figure S12.1. The risk-neutral probability of an up move, p, is given by

$$p = \frac{e^{0.05 \times 3/12} - 0.95}{1.06 - 0.95} = 0.5689$$

There is a payoff from the option of $56.18 - 51 = 5.18$ for the highest final node (which corresponds to two up moves) zero in all other cases. The value of the option is therefore

$$5.18 \times 0.5689^2 \times e^{-0.05 \times 6/12} = 1.635$$

This can also be calculated by working back through the tree as indicated in Figure S12.1. The value of the call option is the lower number at each node in the figure.

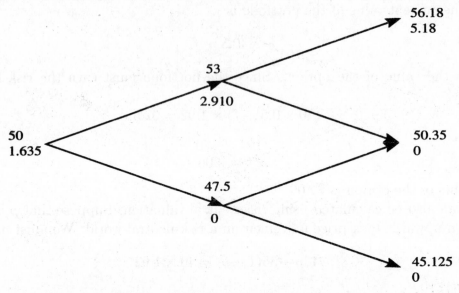

56.18
5.18

53
2.910

50
1.635

50.35
0

47.5
0

45.125
0

Figure S12.1   Tree for Problem 12.12

Problem 12.13.

For the situation considered in Problem 12.12, what is the value of a six-month European put option with a strike price of $51? Verify that the European call and European put prices satisfy put–call parity. If the put option were American, would it ever be optimal to exercise it early at any of the nodes on the tree?

The tree for valuing the put option is shown in Figure S12.2. We get a payoff of $51 - 50.35 = 0.65$ if the middle final node is reached and a payoff of $51 - 45.125 = 5.875$ if the lowest final node is reached. The value of the option is therefore

$$(0.65 \times 2 \times 0.5689 \times 0.4311 + 5.875 \times 0.4311^2)e^{-0.05 \times 6/12} = 1.376$$

This can also be calculated by working back through the tree as indicated in Figure S12.2. The value of the put plus the stock price is from Problem 12.12

$$1.376 + 50 = 51.376$$

The value of the call plus the present value of the strike price is

$$1.635 + 51e^{-0.05 \times 6/12} = 51.376$$

This verifies that put–call parity holds

76

To test whether it worth exercising the option early we compare the value calculated for the option at each node with the payoff from immediate exercise. At node C the payoff from immediate exercise is $51 - 47.5 = 3.5$. Because this is greater than 2.8664, the option should be exercised at this node. The option should not be exercised at either node A or node B.

Figure S12.2   Tree for Problem 12.13

Problem 12.14.

A stock price is currently $25. It is known that at the end of two months it will be either $23 or $27. The risk-free interest rate is 10% per annum with continuous compounding. Suppose S_T is the stock price at the end of two months. What is the value of a derivative that pays off S_T^2 at this time?

At the end of two months the value of the derivative will be either 529 (if the stock price is 23) or 729 (if the stock price is 27). Consider a portfolio consisting of:

$$+\Delta \quad : \quad \text{shares}$$
$$-1 \quad : \quad \text{derivative}$$

The value of the portfolio is either $27\Delta - 729$ or $23\Delta - 529$ in two months. If

$$27\Delta - 729 = 23\Delta - 529$$

i.e.,

$$\Delta = 50$$

the value of the portfolio is certain to be 621. For this value of Δ the portfolio is therefore riskless. The current value of the portfolio is:

$$50 \times 25 - f$$

where f is the value of the derivative. Since the portfolio must earn the risk-free rate of interest

$$(50 \times 25 - f)e^{0.10 \times 2/12} = 621$$

77

i.e.,
$$f = 639.3$$

The value of the option is therefore \$639.3.

This can also be calculated directly from equations (12.2) and (12.3). $u = 1.08$, $d = 0.92$ so that
$$p = \frac{e^{0.10 \times 2/12} - 0.92}{1.08 - 0.92} = 0.6050$$

and
$$f = e^{-0.10 \times 2/12}(0.6050 \times 729 + 0.3950 \times 529) = 639.3$$

Problem 12.15.

Calculate u, d, and p when a binomial tree is constructed to value an option on a foreign currency. The tree step size is one month, the domestic interest rate is 5% per annum, the foreign interest rate is 8% per annum, and the volatility is 12% per annum.

In this case
$$a = e^{(0.05-0.08) \times 1/12} = 0.9975$$

$$u = e^{0.12\sqrt{1/12}} = 1.0352$$

$$d = 1/u = 0.9660$$

$$p = \frac{0.9975 - 0.9660}{1.0352 - 0.9660} = 0.4553$$

CHAPTER 13
Valuing Stock Options:
The Black–Scholes–Merton Model

This is the point at which the book begins to get a little more technical! Chapter 13 presents the pathbreaking stock option pricing model published by Fischer Black, Myron Scholes, and Robert Merton in 1973. The Black-Scholes–Merton model is based on the assumption that the stock price at any future time has a lognormal probability distribution (see Figure 13.1). This assumption is valid in a world where the return on the stock (not the stock price itself) follows a random walk.

The Black–Scholes–Merton model is given by equations (13.5) and (13.6):

$$c = S_0 N(d_1) - K e^{-rT} N(d_2)$$

$$p = K e^{-rT} N(-d_2) - S_0 N(-d_1)$$

where

$$d_1 = \frac{\ln(S_0/K) + (r + \sigma^2/2)T}{\sigma\sqrt{T}}$$

$$d_2 = \frac{\ln(S_0/K) + (r - \sigma^2/2)T}{\sigma\sqrt{T}} = d_1 - \sigma\sqrt{T}$$

In these equations, c and p are the prices of European call and put options on the stock, S_0 is the current stock price, K is the strike price, r is the risk-free rate, σ is the volatility, and T is the time to maturity. The function $N(x)$ is the cumulative probability distribution function for a normally distributed variable with a mean of zero and a standard deviation of 1. (See Figure 13.4.)

The stock is assumed to pay no dividends in the basic Black–Scholes–Merton model. The European option price depends on five variables: S, K, r, σ, and T. Of these, two are properties of the option and therefore known (K and T), two are market variables that can be readily observed (S_0 and r). Only the volatility σ causes any problems when the formula is used. Section 13.3 explains how volatility can be estimated from historical data. Section 13.9 explains how volatility can be implied from the market prices of options.

You should make sure you understand the no-arbitrage arguments in Section 13.6. They are similar to the no-arbitrage arguments used in Chapter 12 to price options when there is one-step binomial tree. The difference is that in this case the portfolio that is set up remains riskless for only a very short (theoretically an infinitesimally short) period of time.

Another important section is Section 13.8. This extends the risk-neutral valuation ideas introduced in Chapter 12. Make sure you understand how risk-neutral valuation can be used to get the

$$f = S_0 - K e^{-rT}$$

formula for valuing a forward contract with delivery price K. The Black–Scholes–Merton formula can be derived using risk-neutral valuation. The methodology is analogous to the methodology for valuing a forward contract with delivery price K, but the math is much more involved.

The last part of the chapter discusses how the Black–Scholes–Merton formula can be modified to allow for dividends. The basic approach is to calculate D, the present value of the dividends that will be paid during the life of the option. The variable S_0 is then replaced by $S_0 - D$ in the Black–Scholes formula. Black's approximation for valuing American call options involves setting the price equal to the greater of the prices of two European call options. The first expires at the same time as the American option; the second expires just before the final ex-dividend date (i.e., the ex-dividend date that is closest to, but before, the American option's maturity).

SOLUTIONS TO PRACTICE QUESTIONS

Problem 13.8.

A stock price is currently $40. Assume that the expected return from the stock is 15% and its volatility is 25%. What is the probability distribution for the rate of return (with continuous compounding) earned over a one-year period?

In this case $\mu = 0.15$ and $\sigma = 0.25$. From equation (13.4) the probability distribution for the rate of return over a one-year period with continuous compounding is:

$$\phi\left(0.15 - \frac{0.25^2}{2},\, 0.25\right)$$

i.e.,

$$\phi(0.11875,\, 0.25)$$

The expected value of the return is 11.875% per annum and the standard deviation is 25.0% per annum.

Problem 13.9.

A stock price has an expected return of 16% and a volatility of 35%. The current price is $38.

    a. *What is the probability that a European call option on the stock with an exercise price of $40 and a maturity date in six months will be exercised?*

    b. *What is the probability that a European put option on the stock with the same exercise price and maturity will be exercised?*

(a) The required probability is the probability of the stock price being above $40 in six months time. Suppose that the stock price in six months is S_T

$$\ln S_T \sim \phi\left(\ln 38 + (0.16 - \frac{0.35^2}{2})0.5,\, 0.35\sqrt{0.5}\right)$$

i.e.,

$$\ln S_T \sim \phi(3.687, 0.247)$$

Since $\ln 40 = 3.689$, the required probability is

$$1 - N\left(\frac{3.689 - 3.687}{0.247}\right) = 1 - N(0.008)$$

From normal distribution tables $N(0.008) = 0.5032$ so that the required probability is 0.4968.

(b) In this case the required probability is the probability of the stock price being less than \$40 in six months time. It is

$$1 - 0.4968 = 0.5032$$

Problem 13.10.

Prove that, with the notation in the chapter, a 95% confidence interval for S_T is between

$$S_0 e^{(\mu - \sigma^2/2)T - 1.96\sigma\sqrt{T}} \quad \text{and} \quad S_0 e^{(\mu - \sigma^2/2)T + 1.96\sigma\sqrt{T}}$$

From equation (13.2):

$$\ln S_T \sim \phi[\ln S_0 + (\mu - \frac{\sigma^2}{2})T, \sigma\sqrt{T}]$$

95% confidence intervals for $\ln S_T$ are therefore

$$\ln S_0 + (\mu - \frac{\sigma^2}{2})T - 1.96\sigma\sqrt{T}$$

and

$$\ln S_0 + (\mu - \frac{\sigma^2}{2})T + 1.96\sigma\sqrt{T}$$

95% confidence intervals for S_T are therefore

$$e^{\ln S_0 + (\mu - \sigma^2/2)T - 1.96\sigma\sqrt{T}} \quad \text{and} \quad e^{\ln S_0 + (\mu - \sigma^2/2)T + 1.96\sigma\sqrt{T}}$$

i.e.

$$S_0 e^{(\mu - \sigma^2/2)T - 1.96\sigma\sqrt{T}} \quad \text{and} \quad S_0 e^{(\mu - \sigma^2/2)T + 1.96\sigma\sqrt{T}}$$

Problem 13.11.

A portfolio manager announces that the average of the returns realized in each of the last 10 years is 20% per annum. In what respect is this statement misleading?

This problem relates to the material in Section 13.2. The statement is misleading in that a certain sum of money, say \$1000, when invested for 10 years in the fund would have realized a return (with annual compounding) of less than 20% per annum.

81

The average of the returns realized in each year is always greater than the return per annum (with annual compounding) realized over 10 years. The first is an arithmetic average of the returns in each year; the second is a geometric average of these returns.

Problem 13.12.

Assume that a non-dividend-paying stock has an expected return of μ and a volatility of σ. An innovative financial institution has just announced that it will trade a derivative that pays off a dollar amount equal to

$$\frac{1}{T} \ln\left(\frac{S_T}{S_0}\right)$$

at time T. The variables S_0 and S_T denote the values of the stock price at time zero and time T.

    a. Describe the payoff from this derivative.

    b. Use risk-neutral valuation to calculate the price of the derivative at time zero.

(a) The derivative will pay off a dollar amount equal to the continuously compounded return on the security between times 0 and T.

(b) The expected value of $\ln(S_T/S_0)$ is, from equation (13.4), $(\mu - \sigma^2/2)T$. The expected payoff from the derivative is therefore $\mu - \sigma^2/2$. In a risk-neutral world this becomes $r - \sigma^2/2$. The value of the derivative at time zero is therefore:

$$\left(r - \frac{\sigma^2}{2}\right)e^{-rT}$$

Problem 13.13.

What is the price of a European call option on a non-dividend-paying stock when the stock price is \$52, the strike price is \$50, the risk-free interest rate is 12% per annum, the volatility is 30% per annum, and the time to maturity is three months?

In this case $S_0 = 52$, $K = 50$, $r = 0.12$, $\sigma = 0.30$ and $T = 0.25$.

$$d_1 = \frac{\ln(52/50) + (0.12 + 0.3^2/2)0.25}{0.30\sqrt{0.25}} = 0.5365$$

$$d_2 = d_1 - 0.30\sqrt{0.25} = 0.3865$$

The price of the European call is

$$52N(0.5365) - 50e^{-0.12\times0.25}N(0.3865)$$

$$= 52 \times 0.7042 - 50e^{-0.03} \times 0.6504$$

$$= 5.06$$

or \$5.06.

82

Problem 13.14.

What is the price of a European put option on a non-dividend-paying stock when the stock price is \$69, the strike price is \$70, the risk-free interest rate is 5% per annum, the volatility is 35% per annum, and the time to maturity is six months?

In this case $S_0 = 69$, $K = 70$, $r = 0.05$, $\sigma = 0.35$ and $T = 0.5$.

$$d_1 = \frac{\ln(69/70) + (0.05 + 0.35^2/2) \times 0.5}{0.35\sqrt{0.5}} = 0.1666$$

$$d_2 = d_1 - 0.35\sqrt{0.5} = -0.0809$$

The price of the European put is

$$70e^{-0.05 \times 0.5} N(0.0809) - 69N(-0.1666)$$

$$= 70e^{-0.025} \times 0.5323 - 69 \times 0.4338$$

$$= 6.40$$

or \$6.40.

$N(.0809) = N(0.9) - .91[N(.09) - N(.08)]$
$= .5359 - .91[.5359 - .5319]$
$= .5323$

$N(-.1666) = N(-.16) - .66[N(0.16) - N(.17)]$
$= .4364 - .66[.4364 - .4325]$
$= .4338$

Problem 13.15.

A call option on a non-dividend-paying stock has a market price of \$2.50. The stock price is \$15, the exercise price is \$13, the time to maturity is three months, and the risk-free interest rate is 5% per annum. What is the implied volatility?

In the case $c = 2.5$, $S_0 = 15$, $K = 13$, $T = 0.25$, $r = 0.05$. The implied volatility must be calculated using an iterative procedure.

A volatility of 0.2 (or 20% per annum) gives $c = 2.20$. A volatility of 0.3 gives $c = 2.32$. A volatility of 0.4 gives $c = 2.507$. A volatility of 0.39 gives $c = 2.487$. By interpolation the implied volatility is about 0.396 or 39.6% per annum.

The implied volatility can also be calculated using DerivaGem. Select equity as the Underlying Type in the first worksheet. Select Analytic European as the Option Type. Input stock price as 15, the risk-free rate as 5%, time to exercise as 0.25, and exercise price as 13. Leave the dividend table blank because we are assuming no dividends. Select the button corresponding to call. Select the implied volatility button. Input the Price as 2.5 in the second half of the option data table. Hit the *Enter* key and click on calculate. DerivaGem will show the volatility of the option as 39.64%.

Problem 13.16.

Show that the Black–Scholes–Merton formula for a call option gives a price that tends to $\max(S_0 - K, 0)$ as $T \to 0$.

$$d_1 = \frac{\ln(S_0/K) + (r + \sigma^2/2)T}{\sigma\sqrt{T}}$$

$$= \frac{\ln(S_0/K)}{\sigma\sqrt{T}} + \frac{r + \sigma^2/2}{\sigma}\sqrt{T}$$

As $T \to 0$, the second term on the right hand side tends to zero. The first term tends to $+\infty$ if $\ln(S_0/K) > 0$ and to $-\infty$ if $\ln(S_0/K) < 0$. Since $\ln(S_0/K) > 0$ when $S_0 > K$ and $\ln(S_0/K) < 0$ when $S_0 < K$, it follows that

$$d_1 \to \infty \text{ as } T \to 0 \text{ when } S_0 > K$$

$$d_1 \to -\infty \text{ as } T \to 0 \text{ when } S_0 < K$$

Similarly

$$d_2 \to \infty \text{ as } T \to 0 \text{ when } S_0 > K$$

$$d_2 \to -\infty \text{ as } T \to 0 \text{ when } S_0 < K$$

Under the Black-Scholes formula the call price, c is given by:

$$c = S_0 N(d_1) - K e^{-rT} N(d_2)$$

From the above results, when $S_0 > K$, $N(d_1) \to 1.0$ and $N(d_2) \to 1.0$ as $T \to 0$ so that $c \to S_0 - K$. Also, when $S_0 < K$, $N(d_1) \to 0$ and $N(d_2) \to 0$ as $T \to 0$ so that $c \to 0$.

These results show that $c \to \max(S_0 - K, 0)$ as $T \to 0$.

Problem 13.17.

Explain carefully why Black's approach to evaluating an American call option on a dividend-paying stock may give an approximate answer even when only one dividend is anticipated. Does the answer given by Black's approach understate or overstate the true option value? Explain your answer.

Black's approach in effect assumes that the holder of option must decide at time zero whether it is a European option maturing at time t_n (the final ex-dividend date) or a European option maturing at time T. In fact the holder of the option has more flexibility than this. The holder can choose to exercise at time t_n if the stock price at that time is above some level but not otherwise. Furthermore, if the option is not exercised at time t_n, it can still be exercised at time T.

It appears that Black's approach should understate the true option value. This is because the holder of the option has more alternative strategies for deciding when to exercise the option than the two strategies implicitly assumed by the approach. These alternative strategies add value to the option.

However, this is not the whole story! The standard approach to valuing either an American or a European option on a stock paying a single dividend applies the volatility to the stock price less the present value of the dividend. (The procedure for valuing an American option is explained in Chapter 18.) Black's approach when considering exercise just prior to the dividend date applies the volatility to the stock price itself. Black's approach therefore assumes more stock price variability than the standard approach in some of its calculations. In some circumstances it can give a higher price than the standard approach.

Problem 13.18.

Consider an American call option on a stock. The stock price is $70, the time to maturity is eight months, the risk-free rate of interest is 10% per annum, the exercise price is $65, and the volatility is 32%. A dividend of $1 is expected after three months and again after six months. Use the results in the appendix to show that it can never be optimal to exercise the option on either of the two dividend dates. Use DerivaGem to calculate the price of the option.

With the notation in the text

$$D_1 = D_2 = 1, \quad t_1 = 0.25, \quad t_2 = 0.50, \quad T = 0.6667, \quad r = 0.1 \quad \text{and} \quad K = 65$$

$$K(1 - e^{-r(T-t_2)}) = 65(1 - e^{-0.1 \times 0.1667}) = 1.07$$

Hence

$$D_2 < K(1 - e^{-r(T-t_2)})$$

Also:

$$K(1 - e^{-r(t_2 - t_1)}) = 65(1 - e^{-0.1 \times 0.25}) = 1.60$$

Hence:

$$D_1 < K(1 - e^{-r(t_2 - t_1)})$$

It follows from the conditions established in the Appendix to Chapter 13 that the option should never be exercised early. The option can therefore be value as a European option. The present value of the dividends is

$$e^{-0.25 \times 0.1} + e^{-0.50 \times 0.1} = 1.9265$$

Also:

$$S_0 = 68.0735, \quad K = 65, \quad \sigma = 0.32, \quad r = 0.1, \quad T = 0.6667$$

$$d_1 = \frac{\ln(68.0735/65) + (0.1 + 0.32^2/2)0.6667}{0.32\sqrt{0.6667}} = 0.5626$$

$$d_2 = d_1 - 0.32\sqrt{0.6667} = 0.3013$$

$$N(d_1) = 0.7131, \quad N(d_2) = 0.6184$$

and the call price is

$$68.0735 \times 0.7131 - 65e^{-0.1 \times 0.6667} \times 0.6184 = 10.94$$

or $10.94.

DerivaGem can be used to calculate the price of this option. Select equity as the Underlying Type in the first worksheet. Select Analytic European as the Option Type. Input stock price as 70, the volatility as 32%, the risk-free rate as 10%, time to exercise as =8/12, and exercise price as 65. In the dividend table, enter the times of dividends as 0.25 and 0.50, and the amounts of the dividends in each case as 1. Select the button corresponding to call. Hit the *Enter* key and click on calculate. DerivaGem will show the value of the option as $10.942.

Problem 13.19.

A stock price is currently $50 and the risk-free interest rate is 5%. Use the DerivaGem software to translate the following table of European call options on the stock into a table of implied volatilities, assuming no dividends. Are the option prices consistent with the assumptions underlying Black–Scholes–Merton?

Strike Price ($)	Maturity (months)		
	3	6	12
45	7.00	8.30	10.50
50	3.50	5.20	7.50
55	1.60	2.90	5.10

Using DerivaGem we obtain the following table of implied volatilities

Strike Price ($)	Maturity (months)		
	3	6	12
45	37.78	34.99	34.02
50	34.15	32.78	32.03
55	31.98	30.77	30.45

To calculate first number, select equity as the Underlying Type in the first worksheet. Select Analytic European as the Option Type. Input stock price as 50, the risk-free rate as 5%, time to exercise as 0.25, and exercise price as 45. Leave the dividend table blank because we are assuming no dividends. Select the button corresponding to call. Select the implied volatility button. Input the Price as 7.0 in the second half of the option data table. Hit the *Enter* key and click on calculate. DerivaGem will show the volatility of the option as 37.78%. Change the strike price and time to exercise and recompute to calculate the rest of the numbers in the table.

The option prices are not exactly consistent with Black–Scholes–Merton. If they were, the implied volatilities would be all the same. We usually find in practice that low strike price options on a stock have significantly higher implied volatilities than high strike price options on the same stock. This phenomenon is discussed in Chapter 19.

Problem 13.20.

Show that the Black–Scholes–Merton formulas for call and put options satisfy put–call parity.

The Black–Scholes–Merton formula for a European call option is

$$c = S_0 N(d_1) - Ke^{-rT} N(d_2)$$

so that

$$c + Ke^{-rT} = S_0 N(d_1) - Ke^{-rT} N(d_2) + Ke^{-rT}$$

or

$$c + Ke^{-rT} = S_0 N(d_1) + Ke^{-rT}[1 - N(d_2)]$$

or

$$c + Ke^{-rT} = S_0 N(d_1) + Ke^{-rT} N(-d_2)$$

The Black–Scholes–Merton formula for a European put option is

$$p = Ke^{-rT} N(-d_2) - S_0 N(-d_1)$$

so that

$$p + S_0 = Ke^{-rT} N(-d_2) - S_0 N(-d_1) + S_0$$

or

$$p + S_0 = Ke^{-rT} N(-d_2) + S_0[1 - N(-d_1)]$$

or

$$p + S_0 = Ke^{-rT} N(-d_2) + S_0 N(d_1)$$

This shows that the put–call parity result

$$c + Ke^{-rT} = p + S_0$$

holds.

Problem 13.21.

Show that the probability that a European call option will be exercised in a risk-neutral world is, with the notation introduced in this chapter, $N(d_2)$. What is an expression for the value of a derivative that pays off \$100 if the price of a stock at time T is greater than K?

The probability that the call option will be exercised is the probability that $S_T > K$ where S_T is the stock price at time T. In a risk neutral world

$$\ln S_T \sim \phi[\ln S_0 + (r - \sigma^2/2)T, \sigma\sqrt{T}]$$

The probability that $S_T > K$ is the same as the probability that $\ln S_T > \ln K$. This is

$$1 - N\left[\frac{\ln K - \ln S_0 - (r - \sigma^2/2)T}{\sigma\sqrt{T}}\right]$$

$$= N \left[\frac{\ln (S_0/K) + (r - \sigma^2/2)T}{\sigma \sqrt{T}} \right]$$

$$= N(d_2)$$

The expected value at time T in a risk neutral world of a derivative security which pays off \$100 when $S_T > K$ is therefore

$$100N(d_2)$$

From risk neutral valuation the value of the security at time t is

$$100e^{-rT} N(d_2)$$

CHAPTER 14
Employee Stock Options

First you should make sure you understand how employee stock options work and why they are different from regular stock options. The main features of a typical stock option arrangement are listed at the beginning of Section 14.1. Employee stock options tend to be exercised earlier than they would be if they were regular stock options because employees are not allowed to sell their options.

Whether employee stock options align the interests of executives and shareholders is somewhat controversial. If the share price of the company goes up, the shareholders do well and so do the executives. However, if the share price goes down the shareholders lose money, but the executives merely fail to make a gain. It can be argued that granting shares rather than options to executives better aligns their interests to the interests of shareholders. A general problem with stock option (or stock) compensation is that executives have more information about the company than the rest of the market and can time their trades (or option exercises) accordingly.

It used to be the case that the cost to the company of granting at-the-money options was not recognized in the company's financial statements. We then went through a period when the cost had to be reported in the footnotes. We are now in the position where the cost must be expensed on the income statement. This has made employee stock option somewhat less popular than it used to be. The type of compensation given to executives is now less driven by the accounting treatment and some companies use nontraditional plans. For example, the strike price sometimes moves up and down with a reference index (such as the S&P 500) so that the company has to outperform the reference index for the options to move in the money.

The most popular approach to valuing employee stock options is to use Black–Scholes–Merton model with the life of the options set equal to the expected time for which the option will remain active. This is the expected time until the option expires. It might expire because a) it is exercised, b) it reaches the end of its life, or c) it is canceled when the employee leaves the company. But, if the early exercise behavior of employees can be modeled, more sophisticated approaches involving binomial trees can be used.

Some companies have in the past engaged in an illegal practice known as backdating. Suppose that the stock price is now $40, but it was $30 three weeks ago. It is tempting to pretend that the decision to issue at-the-money options was made three weeks ago. This increases the value of the options to the recipients without increasing the expense recorded in the company's financial statements. Academic research uncovered the widespread use of this practice. It became less common when the SEC required companies to report option grants within two business days.

SOLUTIONS TO PRACTICE QUESTIONS

Problem 14.8.

Explain how you would do the analysis to produce a chart such as the one in Figure 14.2.

It would be necessary to look at returns on each stock in the sample (possibly adjusted for the returns on the market and the beta of the stock) around the reported employee stock option grant date. One could designate Day 0 as the grant date and look at returns on each stock each day from Day −30 to Day +30. The returns would then be averaged across the stocks.

Problem 14.9.

On May 31 a company's stock price is $70. One million shares are outstanding. An executive exercises 100,000 stock options with a strike price of $50. What is the impact of this on the stock price?

There should be no impact on the stock price because the stock price will already reflect the dilution expected from the executive's exercise decision.

Problem 14.10.

The notes accompanying a company's financial statements say: "Our executive stock options last 10 years and vest after four years. We valued the options granted this year using the Black–Scholes–Merton model with an expected life of 5 years and a volatility of 20%." What does this mean? Discuss the modeling approach used by the company.

The notes indicate that the Black–Scholes–Merton model was used to produce the valuation with T, the option life, being set equal to 5 years and the stock price volatility being set equal to 20%.

Problem 14.11.

A company has granted 500,000 options to its executives. The stock price and strike price are both $40. The options last for 12 years and vest after four years. The company decides to value the options using an expected life of five years and a volatility of 30% per annum. The company pays no dividends and the risk-free rate is 4%. What will the company report as an expense for the options on its income statement?

The options are valued using Black–Scholes–Merton with $S_0 = 40$, $K = 40$, $T = 5$, $\sigma = 0.3$ and $r = 0.04$. The value of each option is $13.585. The total expense reported is $500,000 \times \$13.585$ or $6.792 million.

Problem 14.12.

A company's CFO says: "The accounting treatment of stock options is crazy. We granted 10,000,000 at-the-money stock options to our employees last year when the stock price was $30. We estimated the value of each option on the grant date to be $5. At our year end the stock price had fallen to $4, but we were still stuck with a $50 million charge to the P&L." Discuss.

The problem is that under the current rules the options are valued only once—on the grant date. Arguably it would make sense to treat the options in the same way as other derivatives entered into by the company and revalue them on each reporting date. However, this does not happen under the current rules in the United States unless the options are settled in cash.

$$\ln\left(\frac{40}{40}\right) = \ln 1 = 0 \qquad \Big|\quad .03^2 = .0009 \div 2 = .0005$$
$$+ \ .04$$
$$\overline{.0405}$$

(14.11)

$$S_0 = 40 \quad K = 40 \quad T = 5 \quad \sigma = 0.3 \quad R = 0.04$$

$$d_1 = \frac{\ln\left(\frac{\overset{S_0}{40}}{\underset{K}{40}}\right) + \left[\overset{R}{.04} + 0.3^2/2\right]\overset{5}{\underset{T}{}}}{0.3\sqrt{5}}$$

$$= \frac{0 + (.0405)5}{0.3\,(2.2361)} = \frac{.2025}{.6708} = 0.3019$$

$$d_2 = d_1 - 0.3\sqrt{5}$$
$$= .3019 - .6708 = -.3689$$

$N(d_1)$ for 0.3019	$N(.30) + .19[N(0.302) - N(0.301)]$

$N(.30) = .6179$ $N(0.302) = .6255$ $N(0.301) = .6217$

$.6255 - .6217 = .0038$

$.0038 \times .19 = .0007$

$.6179 + .0007 = .6186$

$N(d_2)$ for $-.3689$

$N(-.36) + .89[N(.37) - N(.36)]$
$= .3594 + .89[.3557 - .3594]$
$= .3594 - .0033 = .3561$

$.3557 - .3594 = -.0037$

Price of European Call

$$40\,N(.3019) - 40\,e^{-.04\times5}\,N(-.3689)$$

$e^{-.04 \times 5} = .8187$

$$40(.6186) - 40(.8187)(.3561)$$

$$24.7440 - 11.6618$$

$$\longrightarrow = 13.0822 \quad \text{value of each option}$$

CHAPTER 15
Options on Stock Indices and Currencies

If you have a good understanding of Chapter 13, this chapter should present few problems. The chapter provides some examples of how index options and foreign currency options are used and then moves on to extend the results from Chapter 13 so that they can be used to value European options on indices and foreign currencies.

As explained in Section 15.1, index put options can be used to provide portfolio insurance (i.e., ensure that the value of a portfolio does not fall below a certain level). The assets underlying the option should equal the beta of the portfolio times the assets being insured. The strike price should be chosen so that when the index equals the strike price the value of portfolio can be expected to be equal to the insured value. (This is a capital asset pricing model calculation.) Section 15.2 introduces range forward contracts. These are products designed to ensure that the exchange rate applicable to a foreign currency transaction in the future lies between two levels. Range forward contracts can be created by buying a put and selling a call (Figure 15.1a) or buying a call and selling a put (Figure 15.1b)

The key material for valuation is in Section 15.3. This shows that, if an investment asset provides a yield at rate q, then the Black–Scholes formula applies for a European option with S_0 replaced by $S_0 e^{-qT}$ (see equations 15.4 and 15.5). What is more, the lower bounds on option prices in Chapter 10 apply with S_0 replaced by $S_0 e^{-qT}$ (see equations 15.1 and 15.2). Also put–call parity applies with S_0 replaced by $S_0 e^{-qT}$ (see equation 15.3).

For American options we must arrange the tree so that on average the asset price grows at $r - q$ rather than r in the risk-neutral world represented by the tree. This means that the growth factor variable a is defined as $e^{(r-q)\Delta t}$ rather than as $e^{r\Delta t}$.

When valuing options on stock indices we set q equal to the average dividend yield on the index during the life of the option. Most exchange-traded options on stock indices are European. An exception is the OEX (American option on the S&P 100).

When valuing options on currencies we set q equal to the foreign risk-free rate, r_f. Make sure you understand why a currency is analogous to an asset providing a known yield. The key point is that interest income on the foreign currency is earned in the foreign currency not the domestic currency. As equations (15.10) and (15.11) show, the pricing formulas for European currency options can be expressed in terms of forward exchange rates rather than spot exchange rates. It is then not necessary to know what the foreign risk-free rate, r_f, is. (All the relevant information about r_f is included in F_0.)

SOLUTIONS TO PRACTICE QUESTIONS

Problem 15.8.

Show that the formula in equation (15.9) for a put option to sell one unit of currency A for currency B at strike price K gives the same value as equation (15.8) for a call option to buy K units of currency B for currency A at a strike price of 1/K.

A put option to sell one unit of currency A for K units of currency B is worth

$$Ke^{-r_B T}N(-d_2) - S_0 e^{-r_A T}N(-d_1)$$

where

$$d_1 = \frac{\ln(S_0/K) + (r_B - r_A + \sigma^2/2)T}{\sigma\sqrt{T}}$$

$$d_2 = \frac{\ln(S_0/K) + (r_B - r_A - \sigma^2/2)T}{\sigma\sqrt{T}}$$

and r_A and r_B are the risk-free rates in currencies A and B, respectively. The value of the option is measured in units of currency B. Defining $S_0^* = 1/S_0$ and $K^* = 1/K$

$$d_1 = \frac{-\ln(S_0^*/K^*) - (r_A - r_B - \sigma^2/2)T}{\sigma\sqrt{T}}$$

$$d_2 = \frac{-\ln(S_0^*/K^*) - (r_A - r_B + \sigma^2/2)T}{\sigma\sqrt{T}}$$

The put price is therefore

$$S_0 K[S_0^* e^{-r_B T}N(d_1^*) - K^* e^{-r_A T}N(d_2^*)]$$

where

$$d_1^* = -d_2 = \frac{\ln(S_0^*/K^*) + (r_A - r_B + \sigma^2/2)T}{\sigma\sqrt{T}}$$

$$d_2^* = -d_1 = \frac{\ln(S_0^*/K^*) + (r_A - r_B - \sigma^2/2)T}{\sigma\sqrt{T}}$$

This shows that put option is equivalent to KS_0 call options to buy 1 unit of currency A for $1/K$ units of currency B. In this case the value of the option is measured in units of currency A. To obtain the call option value in units of currency B (the same units as the value of the put option was measured in) we must divide by S_0. This proves the result.

Problem 15.9.

A foreign currency is currently worth $1.50. The domestic and foreign risk-free interest rates are 5% and 9%, respectively. Calculate a lower bound for the value of a six-month call option on the currency with a strike price of $1.40 if it is (a) European and (b) American.

93

r_f = foreign int. rate
r = domestic rate

Lower bound for European option is

$$c \geq S_0e^{-r_fT} - Ke^{-rT} = 1.5e^{-0.09\times0.5} - 1.4e^{-0.05\times0.5} = 0.069$$

see pg 337

Lower bound for American option is

$$S_0 - K = 0.10$$

$1.50 - 1.40 = 0.10$

Problem 15.10.

Consider a stock index currently standing at 250. The dividend yield on the index is 4% per annum, and the risk-free rate is 6% per annum. A three-month European call option on the index with a strike price of 245 is currently worth \$10. What is the value of a three-month put option on the index with a strike price of 245?

In this case $S_0 = 250$, $q = 0.04$, $r = 0.06$ (risk free), $T = 0.25$, $K = 245$, and $c = 10$. Using put–call parity

$$c + Ke^{-rT} = p + S_0e^{-qT}$$

or

$$p = c + Ke^{-rT} - S_0e^{-qT}$$

Substituting:

$$p = 10 + 245e^{-0.25\times0.06} - 250e^{-0.25\times0.04} = 3.84$$

The put price is 3.84.

Problem 15.11.

An index currently stands at 696 and has a volatility of 30% per annum. The risk-free rate of interest is 7% per annum and the index provides a dividend yield of 4% per annum. Calculate the value of a three-month European put with an exercise price of 700.

In this case $S_0 = 696$, $K = 700$, $r = 0.07$, $\sigma = 0.3$, $T = 0.25$ and $q = 0.04$. The option can be valued using equation (15.5). numerator = .01302

$\ln\left(\frac{696}{700}\right) = -.00573$

$\frac{.09}{2} = .04500$

$.07 - .04 + .045 = .075$

$.075 \times .25 = .01875$

$$d_1 = \frac{\ln(696/700) + (0.07 - 0.04 + 0.09/2)\times 0.25}{0.3\sqrt{0.25}} = 0.0868 \checkmark$$

.08680

$0.3\sqrt{0.25} T = .15$

$$d_2 = d_1 - 0.3\sqrt{0.25} = -0.0632 \checkmark$$

.08680 - .15 =

and

$$N(-d_1) = 0.4654, \quad N(-d_2) = 0.5252$$

The value of the put, p, is given by:

$$p = 700e^{-0.07\times0.25}\times 0.5252 - 696e^{-0.04\times0.25}\times 0.4654 = 40.6$$

i.e., it is \$40.6.

$N(-.0632)$
$= N(-.06) - .32[N(.07) - N(.06)]$
$.4761 + .32[.4721 - .4761]$
$-.00400$
$= .4761 + .00128 =$

94

$N(.0868)$
$= N(.08) + .68[N(.09) - N(.08)]$
$= .5319 + .68[.5359 - .5319]$
$= .5319 + .68[.0040]$
$= .5319 + .00272$
$= .53462$

Problem 15.12.

Show that if C is the price of an American call with exercise price K and maturity T on a stock paying a dividend yield of q, and P is the price of an American put on the same stock with the same strike price and exercise date,

$$S_0 e^{-qT} - K < C - P < S_0 - K e^{-rT}$$

where S_0 is the stock price, r is the risk-free rate, and $r > 0$. (Hint: To obtain the first half of the inequality, consider possible values of:

> Portfolio A: a European call option plus an amount K invested at the risk-free rate
> Portfolio B: an American put option plus e^{-qT} of stock with dividends being reinvested in the stock

To obtain the second half of the inequality, consider possible values of:

> Portfolio C: an American call option plus an amount Ke^{-rT} invested at the risk-free rate
> Portfolio D: a European put option plus one stock with dividends being reinvested in the stock)

Following the hint, we first consider

Portfolio A: A European call option plus an amount K invested at the risk-free rate
Portfolio B: An American put option plus e^{-qT} of stock with dividends being reinvested in the stock.

Portfolio A is worth $c + K$ while portfolio B is worth $P + S_0 e^{-qT}$. If the put option is exercised at time τ $(0 \le \tau < T)$, portfolio B becomes:

$$K - S_\tau + S_\tau e^{-q(T-\tau)} \le K$$

where S_τ is the stock price at time τ. Portfolio A is worth

$$c + K e^{r\tau} \ge K$$

Hence portfolio A is worth at least as much as portfolio B. If both portfolios are held to maturity (time T), portfolio A is worth

$$\max(S_T - K, 0) + K e^{rT}$$
$$= \max(S_T, K) + K(e^{rT} - 1)$$

Portfolio B is worth $\max(S_T, K)$. Hence portfolio A is worth more than portfolio B.

Because portfolio A is worth at least as much as portfolio B in all circumstances

$$P + S_0 e^{-qT} \le c + K$$

Because $c \le C$:

$$P + S_0 e^{-qT} \le C + K$$

or

$$S_0 e^{-qT} - K \le C - P$$

This proves the first part of the inequality.

For the second part consider:

Portfolio C: An American call option plus an amount Ke^{-rT} invested at the risk-free rate

Portfolio D: A European put option plus one stock with dividends being reinvested in the stock.

Portfolio C is worth $C + Ke^{-rT}$ while portfolio D is worth $p + S_0$. If the call option is exercised at time τ $(0 \le \tau < T)$ portfolio C becomes:

$$S_\tau - K + Ke^{-r(T-\tau)} < S_\tau$$

while portfolio D is worth

$$p + S_\tau e^{q(\tau - t)} \ge S_\tau$$

Hence portfolio D is worth more than portfolio C. If both portfolios are held to maturity (time T), portfolio C is worth $\max(S_T, K)$ while portfolio D is worth

$$\max(K - S_T, 0) + S_T e^{qT}$$
$$= \max(S_T, K) + S_T(e^{qT} - 1)$$

Hence portfolio D is worth at least as much as portfolio C.

Since portfolio D is worth at least as much as portfolio C in all circumstances:

$$C + Ke^{-rT} \le p + S_0$$

Since $p \le P$:

$$C + Ke^{-rT} \le P + S_0$$

or

$$C - P \le S_0 - Ke^{-rT}$$

This proves the second part of the inequality. Hence:

$$S_0 e^{-qT} - K \le C - P \le S_0 - Ke^{-rT}$$

Problem 15.13.

Show that a European call option on a currency has the same price as the corresponding European put option on the currency when the forward price equals the strike price.

This follows from put–call parity and the relationship between the forward price, F_0, and the spot price, S_0.

$$c + Ke^{-rT} = p + S_0 e^{-r_f T}$$

and

$$F_0 = S_0 e^{(r - r_f)T}$$

so that

$$c + Ke^{-rT} = p + F_0 e^{-rT}$$

If $K = F_0$ this reduces to $c = p$. The result that $c = p$ when $K = F_0$ is true for options on all underlying assets, not just options on currencies. An at-the-money option is frequently defined as one where $K = F_0$ (or $c = p$) rather than one where $K = S_0$.

Problem 15.14.

Would you expect the volatility of a stock index to be greater or less than the volatility of a typical stock? Explain your answer.

The volatility of a stock index can be expected to be less than the volatility of a typical stock. This is because some risk (i.e., return uncertainty) is diversified away when a portfolio of stocks is created. In capital asset pricing model terminology, there exists systematic and unsystematic risk in the returns from an individual stock. However, in a stock index, unsystematic risk has been diversified away and only the systematic risk contributes to volatility.

Problem 15.15.

Does the cost of portfolio insurance increase or decrease as the beta of a portfolio increases? Explain your answer.

The cost of portfolio insurance increases as the beta of the portfolio increases. This is because portfolio insurance involves the purchase of a put option on the portfolio. As beta increases, the volatility of the portfolio increases causing the cost of the put option to increase. When index options are used to provide portfolio insurance, both the number of options required and the strike price increase as beta increases.

Problem 15.16.

Suppose that a portfolio is worth $60 million and the S&P 500 is at 1200. If the value of the portfolio mirrors the value of the index, what options should be purchased to provide protection against the value of the portfolio falling below $54 million in one year's time?

If the value of the portfolio mirrors the value of the index, the index can be expected to have dropped by 10% when the value of the portfolio drops by 10%. Hence when the value of the portfolio drops to $54 million the value of the index can be expected to be 1080. This indicates that put options with an exercise price of 1080 should be purchased. The options should be on:

$$\frac{60,000,000}{1200} = \$50,000$$

times the index. Each option contract is for $100 times the index. Hence 500 contracts should be purchased.

Problem 15.17.

Consider again the situation in Problem 15.16. Suppose that the portfolio has a beta of 2.0, the risk-free interest rate is 5% per annum, and the dividend yield on both the

97

portfolio and the index is 3% per annum. *What options should be purchased to provide protection against the value of the portfolio falling below $54 million in one year's time?*

When the value of the portfolio falls to $54 million the holder of the portfolio makes a capital loss of 10%. After dividends are taken into account the loss is 7% during the year. This is 12% below the risk-free interest rate. According to the capital asset pricing model:

$$\text{Excess expected return of portfolio above riskless interest rate} = \beta \times \text{Excess expected return of market above riskless interest rate}$$

Therefore, when the portfolio provides a return 12% below the risk-free interest rate, the market's expected return is 6% below the risk-free interest rate. As the index can be assumed to have a beta of 1.0, this is also the excess expected return (including dividends) from the index. The expected return from the index is therefore -1% per annum. Since the index provides a 3% per annum dividend yield, the expected movement in the index is -4%. Thus when the portfolio's value is $54 million the expected value of the index $0.96 \times 1200 = 1152$. Hence European put options should be purchased with an exercise price of 1152. Their maturity date should be in one year.

The number of options required is twice the number required in Problem 15.16. This is because we wish to protect a portfolio which is twice as sensitive to changes in market conditions as the portfolio in Problem 15.16. Hence options on $100,000 (or 1,000 contracts) should be purchased. To check that the answer is correct consider what happens when the value of the portfolio declines by 20% to $48 million. The return including dividends is -17%. This is 22% less than the risk-free interest rate. The index can be expected to provide a return (including dividends) which is 11% less than the risk-free interest rate, i.e. a return of -6%. The index can therefore be expected to drop by 9% to 1092. The payoff from the put options is $(1152 - 1092) \times 100,000 = \$6$ million. This is exactly what is required to restore the value of the portfolio to $54 million.

Problem 15.18.

An index currently stands at 1,500. European call and put options with a strike price of 1,400 and time to maturity of six months have market prices of 154.00 and 34.25, respectively. The six-month risk-free rate is 5%. What is the implied dividend yield?

The implied dividend yield is the value of q that satisfies the put–call parity equation. It is the value of q that solves

$$154 + 1400e^{-0.05 \times 0.5} = 34.25 + 1500e^{-0.5q}$$

This is 1.99%.

Problem 15.19.

A total return index tracks the return, including dividends, on a certain portfolio. Explain how you would value (a) forward contracts and (b) European options on the index.

A total return index behaves like a stock paying no dividends. In a risk-neutral world it can be expected to grow on average at the risk-free rate. Forward contracts and options

98

on total return indices should be valued in the same way as forward contracts and options on non-dividend-paying stocks.

Problem 15.20.

What is the put–call parity relationship for European currency options

The put–call parity relationship for European currency options is

$$c + Ke^{-rT} = p + Se^{-r_f T}$$

To prove this result, the two portfolios to consider are:

Portfolio A: one call option plus one discount bond which will be worth K at time T

Portfolio B: one put option plus $e^{-r_f T}$ of foreign currency invested at the foreign risk-free interest rate.

Both portfolios are worth $\max(S_T, K)$ at time T. They must therefore be worth the same today. The result follows.

Problem 15.21.

Can an option on the yen-euro exchange rate be created from two options, one on the dollar-euro exchange rate, and the other on the dollar-yen exchange rate? Explain your answer.

There is no way of doing this. A natural idea is to create an option to exchange K euros for one yen from an option to exchange Y dollars for 1 yen and an option to exchange K euros for Y dollars. The problem with this is that it assumes that either both options are exercised or that neither option is exercised. There are always some circumstances where the first option is in-the-money at expiration while the second is not and vice versa.

Problem 15.22.

Prove the results in equation (15.1), (15.2), and (15.3) using the portfolios indicated.

In portfolio A, the cash, if it is invested at the risk-free interest rate, will grow to K at time T. If $S_T > K$, the call option is exercised at time T and portfolio A is worth S_T. If $S_T < K$, the call option expires worthless and the portfolio is worth K. Hence, at time T, portfolio A is worth

$$\max(S_T, K)$$

Because of the reinvestment of dividends, portfolio B becomes one share at time T. It is, therefore, worth S_T at this time. It follows that portfolio A is always worth as much as, and is sometimes worth more than, portfolio B at time T. In the absence of arbitrage opportunities, this must also be true today. Hence,

$$c + Ke^{-rT} \geq S_0 e^{-qT}$$

or

$$c \geq S_0 e^{-qT} - Ke^{-rT}$$

This proves equation (15.1)

99

In portfolio C, the reinvestment of dividends means that the portfolio is one put option plus one share at time T. If $S_T < K$, the put option is exercised at time T and portfolio C is worth K. If $S_T > K$, the put option expires worthless and the portfolio is worth S_T. Hence, at time T, portfolio C is worth

$$\max(S_T, K)$$

Portfolio D is worth K at time T. It follows that portfolio C is always worth as much as, and is sometimes worth more than, portfolio D at time T. In the absence of arbitrage opportunities, this must also be true today. Hence,

$$p + S_0 e^{-qT} \geq K e^{-rT}$$

or

$$p \geq K e^{-rT} - S_0 e^{-qT}$$

This proves equation (15.2)

Portfolios A and C are both worth $\max(S_T, K)$ at time T. They must, therefore, be worth the same today, and the put–call parity result in equation (15.3) follows.

CHAPTER 16
Futures Options

The first part of this chapter describes how futures options work. A call futures option is the right to enter into a long futures contract by a certain future date. The cash payoff when the option is exercised is $F - K$ where F is the most recent settlement futures price and K is the strike price. The exerciser also obtains a long futures contract. A put futures option is the right to enter into a short futures contract by a future date. The cash payoff when the option is exercised is $K - F$. The exerciser also obtains a short futures contract. (See Examples 16.1 and 16.2). When the value of the futures contract is taken into account the payoff on a call is the excess of the futures price at the time of exercise over the strike price and the payoff on a put is the excess of the strike price over the futures price at the time of exercise.

It turns out that a futures price can be treated like an asset that provides a yield equal to the risk-free rate, r. The reason is that, because it costs nothing to enter into a futures contract, the contract must on average give zero profit in a risk-neutral world. Hence its expected growth rate in a risk-neutral world must be zero. This is the same as the expected growth rate for an asset providing a yield at rate r.

Bounds for futures options (equations 16.3 and 16.4), put–call parity for futures options (equation 16.1), pricing formulas for European futures options (equations 16.7 and 16.8), and binomial trees for valuing American futures options (equations 16.5 and 16.6) are all exactly the same as in Chapter 15 except that we set $q = r$. In particular, when a binomial tree is constructed for futures options, $a = 1$.

The equations to value European options on futures are known as Black's model. A European option on a futures has the same price as a regular European option on the spot price of an asset when the futures contract and the option expire at the same time. Similarly, a European option on a forward price has the same price as a regular European option on the spot price of an asset when the forward contract and the option expire at the same time. As a result Black's model can be (and frequently is) used to value a European option on the spot price of an asset in terms the futures or forward price of the underlying asset. (See Example 16.5.)

SOLUTIONS TO PRACTICE QUESTIONS

Problem 16.8.

Suppose you buy a put option contract on October gold futures with a strike price of $900 per ounce. Each contract is for the delivery of 100 ounces. What happens if you exercise when the October futures price is $880?

An amount $(900 - 880) \times 100 = \$2,000$ is added to your margin account and you acquire a short futures position obligating you to sell 100 ounces of gold in October. This position is marked to market in the usual way until you choose to close it out.

Problem 16.9.

Suppose you sell a call option contract on April live cattle futures with a strike price of 90 cents per pound. Each contract is for the delivery of 40,000 pounds. What happens if the contract is exercised when the futures price is 95 cents?

In this case an amount $(0.95 - 0.90) \times 40,000 = \$2,000$ is subtracted from your margin account and you acquire a short position in a live cattle futures contract to sell 40,000 pounds of cattle in April. This position is marked to marked in the usual way until you choose to close it out.

Problem 16.10.

Consider a two-month call futures option with a strike price of 40 when the risk-free interest rate is 10% per annum. The current futures price is 47. What is a lower bound for the value of the futures option if it is (a) European and (b) American?

Lower bound if option is European is

$$(F_0 - K)e^{-rT} = (47 - 40)e^{-0.1 \times 2/12} = 6.88$$

Lower bound if option is American is

$$F_0 - K = 7$$

Problem 16.11.

Consider a four-month put futures option with a strike price of 50 when the risk-free interest rate is 10% per annum. The current futures price is 47. What is a lower bound for the value of the futures option if it is (a) European and (b) American?

Lower bound if option is European is

$$(K - F_0)e^{-rT} = (50 - 47)e^{-0.1 \times 4/12} = 2.90$$

Lower bound if option is American is

$$K - F_0 = 3$$

Problem 16.12.

A futures price is currently 60 and its volatility is 30%. The risk-free interest rate is 8% per annum. Use a two-step binomial tree to calculate the value of a six-month European call option on the futures with a strike price of 60? If the call were American, would it ever be worth exercising it early?

In this case $u = e^{0.3 \times \sqrt{1/2}} = 1.1618$; $d = 1/u = 0.0.8607$; and

$$p = \frac{1 - 0.8607}{1.1618 - 0.8607} = 0.4626$$

In the tree shown in Figure S16.1 the middle number at each node is the price of the European option and the lower number is the price of the American option. The tree shows that the value of the European option is 4.3155 and the value of the American option is 4.4026. The American option should sometimes be exercised early.

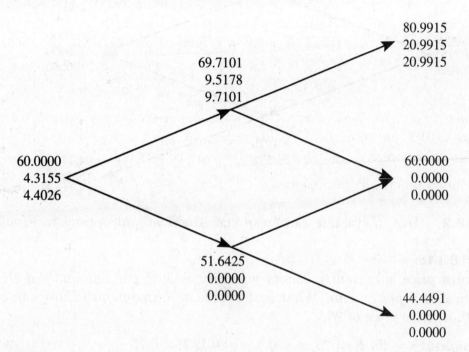

80.9915
20.9915
20.9915

69.7101
9.5178
9.7101

60.0000
4.3155
4.4026

60.0000
0.0000
0.0000

51.6425
0.0000
0.0000

44.4491
0.0000
0.0000

Figure S16.1   Tree to evaluate European and American call options in Problem 16.12.

Problem 16.13.

In Problem 16.12 what does the binomial tree give for a six-month European put option is the value of a six-month European put option on futures with a strike price of 60? If the put were American, would it ever be worth exercising it early? Verify that the call prices calculated in Problem 16.12 and the put prices calculated here satisfy put–call parity relationships.

The parameters u, d and p are the same as in Problem 16.12. The tree in Figure S16.2 shows that the prices of the European and American put options are the same as those calculated for call options in Problem 16.12. This illustrates a symmetry that exists for at-the-money futures options. The American option should sometimes be exercised early. Because $K = F_0$ and $c = p$, the European put–call parity result holds.

$$c + Ke^{-rT} = p + F_0 e^{-rT}$$

Also because $C = P$, $F_0 e^{-rT} < K$, and $Ke^{-rT} < F_0$ the result in equation (16.2) holds. (The first expression in equation (16.2) is negative; the middle expression is zero, and the last expression is positive.

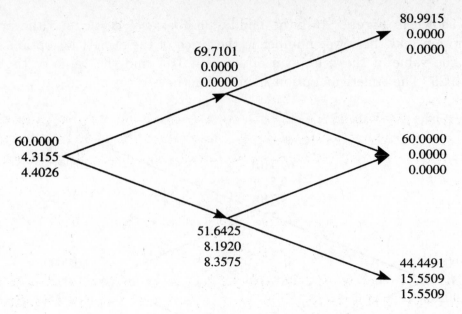

Figure S16.2   Tree to evaluate European and American put options in Problem 16.13.

Problem 16.14.

A futures price is currently 25, its volatility is 30% per annum, and the risk-free interest rate is 10% per annum. What is the value of a nine-month European call on the futures with a strike price of 26?

In this case $F_0 = 25$, $K = 26$, $\sigma = 0.3$, $r = 0.1$, $T = 0.75$

$$d_1 = \frac{\ln(F_0/K) + \sigma^2 T/2}{\sigma\sqrt{T}} = -0.0211$$

$$d_2 = \frac{\ln(F_0/K) - \sigma^2 T/2}{\sigma\sqrt{T}} = -0.2809$$

$$c = e^{-0.075}[25N(-0.0211) - 26N(-0.2809)]$$
$$= e^{-0.075}[25 \times 0.4916 - 26 \times 0.3894] = 2.01$$

Problem 16.15.

A futures price is currently 70, its volatility is 20% per annum, and the risk-free interest rate is 6% per annum. What is the value of a five-month European put on the futures with a strike price of 65?

In this case $F_0 = 70$, $K = 65$, $\sigma = 0.2$, $r = 0.06$, $T = 0.4167$

$$d_1 = \frac{\ln(F_0/K) + \sigma^2 T/2}{\sigma\sqrt{T}} = 0.6386$$

$$d_2 = \frac{\ln(F_0/K) - \sigma^2 T/2}{\sigma\sqrt{T}} = 0.5095$$

$$p = e^{-0.025}[65N(-0.5095) - 70N(-0.6386)]$$
$$= e^{-0.025}[65 \times 0.3052 - 70 \times 0.2615] = 1.495$$

Problem 16.16.

Suppose that a one-year futures price is currently 35. A one-year European call option and a one-year European put option on the futures with a strike price of 34 are both priced at 2 in the market. The risk-free interest rate is 10% per annum. Identify an arbitrage opportunity.

See Eg. 16.1
Pg. 347

In this case

$$c + Ke^{-rT} = 2 + 34e^{-0.1 \times 1} = 32.76$$
$$p + F_0 e^{-rT} = 2 + 35e^{-0.1 \times 1} = 33.67$$

Put-call parity shows that we should buy one call, short one put and short a futures contract. This costs nothing up front. In one year, either we exercise the call or the put is exercised against us. In either case, we buy the asset for 34 and close out the futures position. The gain on the short futures position is $35 - 34 = 1$.

Problem 16.17.

"The price of an at-the-money European call futures option always equals the price of a similar at-the-money European put futures option." Explain why this statement is true.

The put price is

$$e^{-rT}[KN(-d_2) - F_0 N(-d_1)]$$

Because $N(-x) = 1 - N(x)$ for all x the put price can also be written

$$e^{-rT}[K - KN(d_2) - F_0 + F_0 N(d_1)]$$

Because $F_0 = K$ this is the same as the call price:

$$e^{-rT}[F_0 N(d_1) - KN(d_2)]$$

This result can also be proved from put–call parity showing that it is not model dependent.

Problem 16.18.

Suppose that a futures price is currently 30. The risk-free interest rate is 5% per annum. A three-month American call futures option with a strike price of 28 is worth 4. Calculate bounds for the price of a three-month American put futures option with a strike price of 28.

From equation (16.2), $C - P$ must lie between

$$30e^{-0.05 \times 3/12} - 28 = 1.63$$

and

$$30 - 28e^{-0.05 \times 3/12} = 2.35$$

105

Because $C = 4$ we must have $1.63 < 4 - P < 2.35$ or

$$1.65 < P < 2.37$$

Problem 16.19.

Show that if C is the price of an American call option on a futures contract when the strike price is K and the maturity is T, and P is the price of an American put on the same futures contract with the same strike price and exercise date,

$$F_0 e^{-rT} - K < C - P < F_0 - K e^{-rT}$$

where F_0 is the futures price and r is the risk-free rate. Assume that $r > 0$ and that there is no difference between forward and futures contracts. (Hint: Use an analogous approach to that indicated for Problem 15.12.)

In this case we consider

Portfolio A: A European call option on futures plus an amount K invested at the risk-free interest rate

Portfolio B: An American put option on futures plus an amount $F_0 e^{-rT}$ invested at the risk-free interest rate plus a long futures contract maturing at time T.

Following the arguments in Chapter 5 we will treat all futures contracts as forward contracts. Portfolio A is worth $c + K$ while portfolio B is worth $P + F_0 e^{-rT}$. If the put option is exercised at time τ $(0 \leq \tau < T)$, portfolio B is worth

$$K - F_\tau + F_0 e^{-r(T-\tau)} + F_\tau - F_0$$
$$= K + F_0 e^{-r(T-\tau)} - F_0 < K$$

at time τ where F_τ is the futures price at time τ. Portfolio A is worth

$$c + K e^{r\tau} \geq K$$

Hence Portfolio A more than Portfolio B. If both portfolios are held to maturity (time T), Portfolio A is worth

$$\max(F_T - K, 0) + K e^{rT}$$
$$= \max(F_T, K) + K(e^{rT} - 1)$$

Portfolio B is worth

$$\max(K - F_T, 0) + F_0 + F_T - F_0 = \max(F_T, K)$$

Hence portfolio A is worth more than portfolio B.

Because portfolio A is worth more than portfolio B in all circumstances:

$$P + F_0 e^{-r(T-t)} < c + K$$

Because $c \le C$ it follows that

$$P + F_0 e^{-rT} < C + K$$

or

$$F_0 e^{-rT} - K < C - P$$

This proves the first part of the inequality.

For the second part of the inequality consider:

Portfolio C: An American call futures option plus an amount Ke^{-rT} invested at the risk-free interest rate

Portfolio D: A European put futures option plus an amount F_0 invested at the risk-free interest rate plus a long futures contract.

Portfolio C is worth $C + Ke^{-rT}$ while portfolio D is worth $p + F_0$. If the call option is exercised at time τ $(0 \le \tau < T)$ portfolio C becomes:

$$F_\tau - K + Ke^{-r(T-\tau)} < F_\tau$$

while portfolio D is worth

$$p + F_0 e^{r\tau} + F_\tau - F_0$$
$$= p + F_0(e^{r\tau} - 1) + F_\tau \ge F_\tau$$

Hence portfolio D is worth more than portfolio C. If both portfolios are held to maturity (time T), portfolio C is worth $\max(F_T, K)$ while portfolio D is worth

$$\max(K - F_T, 0) + F_0 e^{rT} + F_T - F_0$$
$$= \max(K, F_T) + F_0(e^{rT} - 1)$$
$$> \max(K, F_T)$$

Hence portfolio D is worth more than portfolio C.

Because portfolio D is worth more than portfolio C in all circumstances

$$C + Ke^{-rT} < p + F_0$$

Because $p \le P$ it follows that

$$C + Ke^{-rT} < P + F_0$$

or

$$C - P < F_0 - Ke^{-rT}$$

This proves the second part of the inequality. The result:

$$F_0 e^{-rT} - K < C - P < F_0 - Ke^{-rT}$$

has therefore been proved.

Problem 16.20.

Calculate the price of a three-month European call option on the spot price of silver. The three-month futures price is $12, the strike price is $13, the risk-free rate is 4%, and the volatility of the price of silver is 25%.

This has the same value as a three-month call option on silver futures where the futures contract expires in three months. It can therefore be valued using equation (16.7) with $F_0 = 12$, $K = 13$, $r = 0.04$, $\sigma = 0.25$ and $T = 0.25$. The value is 0.244.

107

CHAPTER 17
The Greek Letters

This chapter considers a trader working as an options market maker at a bank or at an exchange. The trader is responsible for trading financial instruments that depend on one particular market variable (e.g the sterling–dollar exchange rate). The chapter covers the approaches used by the trader to manage risk.

The trader must monitor a number of risk measures (known as "Greek letters") and try to ensure that they remain within reasonable bounds. The most important Greek letter is delta. This is the rate of change of the value of the trader's portfolio with respect to the market variable. The trader can make delta zero by doing a trade in the underlying asset. Suppose for example that the trader responsible for the sterling–dollar exchange rate has a portfolio with a delta of –100,000 when the exchange rate is 1.90. This means that the portfolio increases in value by $-100,000 \times 0.01 = -\$1000$ when the exchange rate increases from 1.90 to 1.91. Delta can be changed to zero by buying 100,000 pounds sterling. A portfolio with a delta of zero is known as a delta-neutral portfolio.

Option traders usually make their portfolios delta neutral (or close to delta neutral) as a matter of course at the end of each day. This is known as rebalancing the portfolio. It makes their portfolios relatively insensitive to small changes in the underlying market variable (the dollar–sterling exchange rate in our example). Tables 17.2 and 17.3 provide examples of how a trader with a portfolio consisting of a single option might fare if the portfolio is rebalanced, bringing delta to zero, every week. You should study these tables carefully and make sure you understand them. The process of bringing delta to zero at regular intervals is known as delta hedging. It underlies the no arbitrage argument for pricing options.

Delta hedging provides protection against small changes in the underlying variable. Gamma measures a trader's exposure to large jumps. Gamma is defined as the rate of change of delta with respect to the underlying variable. Figure 17.7 illustrates how gamma risk arises. The value of the option is assumed to move from C to C' when delta hedging is used. In fact it moves from C to C''.

Vega measures the sensitivity of a portfolio to changes in volatility. Both gamma and vega can be changed only by taking a position in an option. Taking a position in the underlying asset has no impact on gamma and vega. As explained in Business Snapshot 17.1 traders tend to manage gamma and vega opportunistically.

Other Greek letters covered in the chapter are theta (sensitivity to the passage of time) and rho (sensitivity to interest rates). These tend to be less important than delta, gamma, and vega.

The last part of the chapter covers portfolio insurance and the creation of options synthetically. When we wish to hedge an option we use a trading strategy that neutralizes delta (as in Tables 17.2 and 17.3). When we wish to create an option synthetically we use a trading strategy that matches the delta of the option we are trying to create. As explained in Section 17.13 the creation of a synthetic put option on a portfolio of stocks involves buying stocks (or index futures) just after a price rise and selling stocks (or index futures) just after a price fall. As traders found in October 1987, if too many portfolio managers are attempting to create put options synthetically at the same time, the strategy may not produce the desired results.

SOLUTIONS TO PRACTICE QUESTIONS

Problem 17.8.

What does it mean to assert that the theta of an option position is −0.1 when time is measured in years? If a trader feels that neither a stock price nor its implied volatility will change, what type of option position is appropriate?

A theta of −0.1 means that if Δt units of time pass with no change in either the stock price or its volatility, the value of the option declines by $0.1\Delta t$. A trader who feels that neither the stock price nor its implied volatility will change should write an option with as high a negative theta as possible. Relatively short-life at-the-money options have the most negative thetas.

Problem 17.9.

The Black–Scholes price of an out-of-the-money call option with an exercise price of $40 is $4. A trader who has written the option plans to use a stop-loss strategy. The trader's plan is to buy at $40.10 and to sell at $39.90. Estimate the expected number of times the stock will be bought or sold.

The strategy costs the trader 0.10 each time the stock is bought or sold. The total expected cost of the strategy, in present value terms, must be $4. This means that the expected number of times the stock will be bought or sold is approximately 40. The expected number of times it will be bought is approximately 20 and the expected number of times it will be sold is also approximately 20. The buy and sell transactions can take place at any time during the life of the option. The above numbers are therefore only approximately correct because of the effects of discounting. Also the estimate is of the number of times the stock is bought or sold in the risk-neutral world, not the real world.

Problem 17.10.

Suppose that a stock price is currently $20 and that a call option with an exercise price of $25 is created synthetically using a continually changing position in the stock. Consider the following two scenarios:
  a. Stock price increases steadily from $20 to $35 during the life of the option.
  b. Stock price oscillates wildly, ending up at $35.
  Which scenario would make the synthetically created option more expensive? Explain your answer.

The holding of the stock at any given time must be $N(d_1)$. Hence the stock is bought just after the price has risen and sold just after the price has fallen. (This is the buy high sell low strategy referred to in the text.) In the first scenario the stock is continually bought. In second scenario the stock is bought, sold, bought again, sold again, etc. The final holding is the same in both scenarios. The buy, sell, buy, sell... situation clearly leads to higher costs than the buy, buy, buy... situation. This problem emphasizes one disadvantage of creating options synthetically. Whereas the cost of an option that is purchased is known up front and depends on the forecasted volatility, the cost of an option that is created synthetically is not known up front and depends on the volatility actually encountered.

Problem 17.11.

What is the delta of a short position in 1,000 European call options on silver futures? The options mature in eight months, and the futures contract underlying the option matures in nine months. The current nine-month futures price is $8 per ounce, the exercise price of the options is $8, the risk-free interest rate is 12% per annum, and the volatility of silver is 18% per annum.

The delta of a European futures call option is usually defined as the rate of change of the option price with respect to the futures price (not the spot price). It is

$$e^{-rT}N(d_1)$$

In this case $F_0 = 8$, $K = 8$, $r = 0.12$, $\sigma = 0.18$, $T = 0.6667$

$$d_1 = \frac{\ln(8/8) + (0.18^2/2) \times 0.6667}{0.18\sqrt{0.6667}} = 0.0735$$

$N(d_1) = 0.5293$ and the delta of the option is

$$e^{-0.12 \times 0.6667} \times 0.5293 = 0.4886$$

The delta of a short position in 1,000 futures options is therefore -488.6.

Problem 17.12.

In Problem 17.11, what initial position in nine-month silver futures is necessary for delta hedging? If silver itself is used, what is the initial position? If one-year silver futures are used, what is the initial position? Assume no storage costs for silver.

In order to answer this problem it is important to distinguish between the rate of change of the option with respect to the futures price and the rate of change of its price with respect to the spot price.

The former will be referred to as the futures delta; the latter will be referred to as the spot delta. The futures delta of a nine-month futures contract to buy one ounce of silver is by definition 1.0. Hence, from the answer to Problem 17.11, a long position in nine-month futures on 488.6 ounces is necessary to hedge the option position.

The spot delta of a nine-month futures contract is $e^{0.12 \times 0.75} = 1.094$ assuming no storage costs. (This is because silver can be treated in the same way as a non-dividend-paying stock when there are no storage costs. $F_0 = S_0 e^{rT}$ so that the spot delta is the futures delta times e^{rT}) Hence the spot delta of the option position is $-488.6 \times 1.094 = -534.6$. Thus a long position in 534.6 ounces of silver is necessary to hedge the option position.

The spot delta of a one-year silver futures contract to buy one ounce of silver is $e^{0.12} = 1.1275$. Hence a long position in $e^{-0.12} \times 534.6 = 474.1$ ounces of one-year silver futures is necessary to hedge the option position.

Problem 17.13.

A company uses delta hedging to hedge a portfolio of long positions in put and call options on a currency. Which of the following would give the most favorable result?

  a. *A virtually constant spot rate*
  b. *Wild movements in the spot rate*

Explain your answer.

A long position in either a put or a call option has a positive gamma. From Figure 17.8, when gamma is positive the hedger gains from a large change in the stock price and loses from a small change in the stock price. Hence the hedger will fare better in case (b).

Problem 17.14.

Repeat Problem 17.13 for a financial institution with a portfolio of short positions in put and call options on a currency.

A short position in either a put or a call option has a negative gamma. From Figure 17.8, when gamma is negative the hedger gains from a small change in the stock price and loses from a large change in the stock price. Hence the hedger will fare better in case (a).

Problem 17.15.

A financial institution has just sold 1,000 seven-month European call options on the Japanese yen. Suppose that the spot exchange rate is 0.80 cent per yen, the exercise price is 0.81 cent per yen, the risk-free interest rate in the United States is 8% per annum, the risk-free interest rate in Japan is 5% per annum, and the volatility of the yen is 15% per annum. Calculate the delta, gamma, vega, theta, and rho of the financial institution's position. Interpret each number.

In this case $S_0 = 0.80$, $K = 0.81$, $r = 0.08$, $r_f = 0.05$, $\sigma = 0.15$, $T = 0.5833$

$$d_1 = \frac{\ln(0.80/0.81) + \left(0.08 - 0.05 + 0.15^2/2\right) \times 0.5833}{0.15\sqrt{0.5833}} = 0.1016$$

$$d_2 = d_1 - 0.15\sqrt{0.5833} = -0.0130$$

$$N(d_1) = 0.5405; \quad N(d_2) = 0.4998$$

The delta of one call option is $e^{-r_f T}N(d_1) = e^{-0.05 \times 0.5833} \times 0.5405 = 0.5250$.

$$N'(d_1) = \frac{1}{\sqrt{2\pi}}e^{-d_1^2/2} = \frac{1}{\sqrt{2\pi}}e^{-0.00516} = 0.3969$$

so that the gamma of one call option is

$$\frac{N'(d_1)e^{-r_f T}}{S_0 \sigma \sqrt{T}} = \frac{0.3969 \times 0.9713}{0.80 \times 0.15 \times \sqrt{0.5833}} = 4.206$$

The vega of one call option is

$$S_0\sqrt{T}N'(d_1)e^{-r_f T} = 0.80\sqrt{0.5833} \times 0.3969 \times 0.9713 = 0.2355$$

The theta of one call option is

$$-\frac{S_0 N'(d_1)\sigma e^{-r_f T}}{2\sqrt{T}} + r_f S_0 N(d_1)e^{-r_f T} - rKe^{-rT}N(d_2)$$

$$= -\frac{0.8 \times 0.3969 \times 0.15 \times 0.9713}{2\sqrt{0.5833}}$$

$$+ 0.05 \times 0.8 \times 0.5405 \times 0.9713 - 0.08 \times 0.81 \times 0.9544 \times 0.4948$$

$$= -0.0399$$

The rho of one call option is

$$KTe^{-rT}N(d_2)$$
$$= 0.81 \times 0.5833 \times 0.9544 \times 0.4948$$
$$= 0.2231$$

Delta can be interpreted as meaning that, when the spot price increases by a small amount (measured in cents), the value of an option to buy one yen increases by 0.525 times that amount. Gamma can be interpreted as meaning that, when the spot price increases by a small amount (measured in cents), the delta increases by 4.206 times that amount. Vega can be interpreted as meaning that, when the volatility (measured in decimal form) increases by a small amount, the option's value increases by 0.2355 times that amount. When volatility increases by 1% (= 0.01) the option price increases by 0.002355. Theta can be interpreted as meaning that, when a small amount of time (measured in years) passes, the option's value decreases by 0.0399 times that amount. In particular when one calendar day passes it decreases by $0.0399/365 = 0.000109$. Finally, rho can be interpreted as meaning that, when the interest rate (measured in decimal form) increases by a small amount the option's value increases by 0.2231 times that amount. When the interest rate increases by 1% (= 0.01), the options value increases by 0.002231.

Problem 17.16.
Under what circumstances is it possible to make a European option on a stock index both gamma neutral and vega neutral by adding a position in one other European option?

Assume that S_0, K, r, σ, T, q are the parameters for the option held and S_0, K^*, r, σ, T^*, q are the parameters for another option. Suppose that d_1 has its usual meaning and is calculated on the basis of the first set of parameters while d_1^* is the value of d_1 calculated on the basis of the second set of parameters. Suppose further that w of the second option are held for each of the first option held. The gamma of the portfolio is:

$$\alpha \left[\frac{N'(d_1)e^{-qT}}{S_0 \sigma \sqrt{T}} + w \frac{N'(d_1^*)e^{-qT^*}}{S_0 \sigma \sqrt{T^*}} \right]$$

where α is the number of the first option held.

Since we require gamma to be zero:

$$w = -\frac{N'(d_1)e^{-q(T-T^*)}}{N'(d_1^*)} \sqrt{\frac{T^*}{T}}$$

The vega of the portfolio is:

$$\alpha \left[S_0 \sqrt{T} N'(d_1)e^{-q(T)} + w S_0 \sqrt{T^*} N'(d_1^*)e^{-q(T^*)} \right]$$

Since we require vega to be zero:

$$w = -\sqrt{\frac{T}{T^*}} \frac{N'(d_1)e^{-q(T-T^*)}}{N'(d_1^*)}$$

Equating the two expressions for w

$$T^* = T$$

Hence the maturity of the option held must equal the maturity of the option used for hedging.

Problem 17.17.

A fund manager has a well-diversified portfolio that mirrors the performance of the S&P 500 and is worth $360 million. The value of the S&P 500 is 1,200, and the portfolio manager would like to buy insurance against a reduction of more than 5% in the value of the portfolio over the next six months. The risk-free interest rate is 6% per annum. The dividend yield on both the portfolio and the S&P 500 is 3%, and the volatility of the index is 30% per annum.

  a. If the fund manager buys traded European put options, how much would the insurance cost?

  b. Explain carefully alternative strategies open to the fund manager involving traded European call options, and show that they lead to the same result.

  c. If the fund manager decides to provide insurance by keeping part of the portfolio in risk-free securities, what should the initial position be?

  d. If the fund manager decides to provide insurance by using nine-month index futures, what should the initial position be?

The fund is worth $300,000 times the value of the index. When the value of the portfolio falls by 5% (to $342 million), the value of the S&P 500 also falls by 5% to 1140.

The fund manager therefore requires European put options on 300,000 times the S&P 500 with exercise price 1140.

(a) $S_0 = 1200$, $K = 1140$, $r = 0.06$, $\sigma = 0.30$, $T = 0.50$ and $q = 0.03$. Hence:

$$d_1 = \frac{\ln(1200/1140) + (0.06 - 0.03 + 0.3^2/2) \times 0.5}{0.3\sqrt{0.5}} = 0.4186$$

$$d_2 = d_1 - 0.3\sqrt{0.5} = 0.2064$$

$$N(d_1) = 0.6622; \quad N(d_2) = 0.5818$$

$$N(-d_1) = 0.3378; \quad N(-d_2) = 0.4182$$

The value of one put option is

$$1140e^{-rT}N(-d_2) - 1200e^{-qT}N(-d_1)$$
$$= 1140e^{-0.06\times0.5} \times 0.4182 - 1200e^{-0.03\times0.5} \times 0.3378$$
$$= 63.40$$

The total cost of the insurance is therefore

$$300,000 \times 63.40 = \$19,020,000$$

(b) From put–call parity

$$S_0 e^{-qT} + p = c + Ke^{-rT}$$

or:

$$p = c - S_0 e^{-qT} + Ke^{-rT}$$

This shows that a put option can be created by selling (or shorting) e^{-qT} of the index, buying a call option and investing the remainder at the risk-free rate of interest. Applying this to the situation under consideration, the fund manager should:

1) Sell $360e^{-0.03\times0.5} = \$354.64$ million of stock
2) Buy call options on 300,000 times the S&P 500 with exercise price 1140 and maturity in six months.
3) Invest the remaining cash at the risk-free interest rate of 6% per annum.

This strategy gives the same result as buying put options directly.

(c) The delta of one put option is

$$e^{-qT}[N(d_1) - 1]$$
$$= e^{-0.03\times0.5}(0.6622 - 1)$$
$$- 0.3327$$

This indicates that 33.27% of the portfolio (i.e., \$119.77 million) should be initially sold and invested in risk-free securities.

114

(d) The delta of a nine-month index futures contract is

$$e^{(r-q)T} = e^{0.03 \times 0.75} = 1.023$$

The spot short position required is

$$\frac{119,770,000}{1200} = 99,808$$

times the index. Hence a short position in

$$\frac{99,808}{1.023 \times 250} = 390$$

futures contracts is required.

Problem 17.18.

Repeat Problem 17.17 on the assumption that the portfolio has a beta of 1.5. Assume that the dividend yield on the portfolio is 4% per annum.

When the value of the portfolio goes down 5% in six months, the total return from the portfolio, including dividends, in the six months is

$$-5 + 2 = -3\%$$

i.e., -6% per annum. This is 12% per annum less than the risk-free interest rate. Since the portfolio has a beta of 1.5 we would expect the market to provide a return of 8% per annum less than the risk-free interest rate, i.e., we would expect the market to provide a return of -2% per annum. Since dividends on the market index are 3% per annum, we would expect the market index to have dropped at the rate of 5% per annum or 2.5% per six months; i.e., we would expect the market to have dropped to 1170. A total of $450,000 = (1.5 \times 300,000)$ put options on the S&P 500 with exercise price 1170 and exercise date in six months are therefore required.

(a) $S_0 = 1200$, $K = 1170$, $r = 0.06$, $\sigma = 0.3$, $T = 0.5$ and $q = 0.03$. Hence

$$d_1 = \frac{\ln(1200/1170) + (0.06 - 0.03 + 0.09/2) \times 0.5}{0.3\sqrt{0.5}} = 0.2961$$

$$d_2 = d_1 - 0.3\sqrt{0.5} = 0.0840$$

$$N(d_1) = 0.6164; \quad N(d_2) = 0.5335$$

$$N(-d_1) = 0.3836; \quad N(-d_2) = 0.4665$$

The value of one put option is

$$Ke^{-rT}N(-d_2) - S_0e^{-qT}N(-d_1)$$
$$= 1170e^{-0.06 \times 0.5} \times 0.4665 - 1200e^{-0.03 \times 0.5} \times 0.3836$$
$$= 76.28$$

115

The total cost of the insurance is therefore

$$450,000 \times 76.28 = \$34,326,000$$

Note that this is significantly greater than the cost of the insurance in Problem 17.17.

(b) As in Problem 17.17 the fund manager can 1) sell \$354.64 million of stock, 2) buy call options on 450,000 times the S&P 500 with exercise price 1170 and exercise date in six months and 3) invest the remaining cash at the risk-free interest rate.

(c) The portfolio is 50% more volatile than the S&P 500. When the insurance is considered as an option on the portfolio the parameters are as follows: $S_0 = 360$, $K = 342$, $r = 0.06$, $\sigma = 0.45$, $T = 0.5$ and $q = 0.04$

$$d_1 = \frac{\ln{(360/342)} + (0.06 - 0.04 + 0.45^2/2) \times 0.5}{0.45\sqrt{0.5}} = 0.3517$$

$$N(d_1) = 0.6374$$

The delta of the option is

$$e^{-qT}[N(d_1) - 1]$$
$$= e^{-0.04 \times 0.5}(0.6374 - 1)$$
$$= -0.355$$

This indicates that 35.5% of the portfolio (i.e., \$127.8 million) should be sold and invested in riskless securities.

(d) We now return to the situation considered in (a) where put options on the index are required. The delta of each put option is

$$e^{-qT}(N(d_1) - 1)$$
$$= e^{-0.03 \times 0.5}(0.6164 - 1)$$
$$= -0.3779$$

The delta of the total position required in put options is $-450,000 \times 0.3779 = -170,000$. The delta of a nine month index futures is (see Problem 17.17) 1.023. Hence a short position in

$$\frac{170,000}{1.023 \times 250} = 665$$

index futures contracts.

Problem 17.19.

Show by substituting for the various terms in equation (17.4) that the equation is true for:
  a. *A single European call option on a non-dividend-paying stock*
  b. *A single European put option on a non-dividend-paying stock*

c. Any portfolio of European put and call options on a non-dividend-paying stock

(a) For a call option on a non-dividend-paying stock

$$\Delta = N(d_1)$$

$$\Gamma = \frac{N'(d_1)}{S_0\sigma\sqrt{T}}$$

$$\Theta = -\frac{S_0 N'(d_1)\sigma}{2\sqrt{T}} - rKe^{-rT}N(d_2)$$

Hence the left-hand side of equation (17.4) is:

$$= -\frac{S_0 N'(d_1)\sigma}{2\sqrt{T}} - rKe^{-rT}N(d_2) + rS_0 N(d_1) + \frac{1}{2}\sigma S_0 \frac{N'(d_1)}{\sqrt{T}}$$

$$= r[S_0 N(d_1) - Ke^{-rT}N(d_2)]$$

$$= r\Pi$$

(b) For a put option on a non-dividend-paying stock

$$\Delta = N(d_1) - 1 = -N(-d_1)$$

$$\Gamma = \frac{N'(d_1)}{S_0\sigma\sqrt{T}}$$

$$\Theta = -\frac{S_0 N'(d_1)\sigma}{2\sqrt{T}} + rKe^{-rT}N(-d_2)$$

Hence the left-hand side of equation (17.4) is:

$$-\frac{S_0 N'(d_1)\sigma}{2\sqrt{T}} + rKe^{-rT}N(-d_2) - rS_0 N(-d_1) + \frac{1}{2}\sigma S_0 \frac{N'(d_1)}{\sqrt{T}}$$

$$= r[Ke^{-rT}N(-d_2) - S_0 N(-d_1)]$$

$$= r\Pi$$

(c) For a portfolio of options, Π, Δ, Θ and Γ are the sums of their values for the individual options in the portfolio. It follows that equation (17.4) is true for any portfolio of European put and call options.

Problem 17.20.

Suppose that $70 billion of equity assets are the subject of portfolio insurance schemes. Assume that the schemes are designed to provide insurance against the value of the assets declining by more than 5% within one year. Making whatever estimates you find necessary, use the DerivaGem software to calculate the value of the stock or futures contracts that the administrators of the portfolio insurance schemes will attempt to sell if the market falls by 23% in a single day.

We can regard the position of all portfolio insurers taken together as a single put option. The three known parameters of the option, before the 23% decline, are $S_0 = 70$, $K = 66.5$, $T = 1$. Other parameters can be estimated as $r = 0.06$, $\sigma = 0.25$ and $q = 0.03$. Then:

$$d_1 = \frac{\ln(70/66.5) + (0.06 - 0.03 + 0.25^2/2)}{0.25} = 0.4502$$

$$N(d_1) = 0.6737$$

The delta of the option is

$$e^{-qT}[N(d_1) - 1]$$
$$= e^{-0.03}(0.6737 - 1)$$
$$= -0.3167$$

This shows that 31.67% or \$22.17 billion of assets should have been sold before the decline. These numbers can also be produced from DerivaGem by selecting Underlying Type and Index and Option Type as Analytic European.

After the decline, $S_0 = 53.9$, $K = 66.5$, $T = 1$, $r = 0.06$, $\sigma = 0.25$ and $q = 0.03$.

$$d_1 = \frac{\ln(53.9/66.5) + (0.06 - 0.03 + 0.25^2/2)}{0.25} = -0.5953$$

$$N(d_1) = 0.2758$$

The delta of the option has dropped to

$$e^{-0.03 \times 0.5}(0.2758 - 1)$$
$$= -0.7028$$

This shows that cumulatively 70.28% of the assets originally held should be sold. An additional 38.61% of the original portfolio should be sold. The sales measured at pre-crash prices are about \$27.0 billion. At post crash prices they are about 20.8 billion.

Problem 17.21.

Does a forward contract on a stock index have the same delta as the corresponding futures contract? Explain your answer.

With our usual notation the value of a forward contract on the asset is $S_0 e^{-qT} - Ke^{-rT}$. When there is a small change, ΔS, in S_0 the value of the forward contract changes by $e^{-qT}\Delta S$. The delta of the forward contract is therefore e^{-qT}. The futures price is $S_0 e^{(r-q)T}$. When there is a small change, ΔS, in S_0 the futures price changes by $\Delta S e^{(r-q)T}$. Given the daily settlement procedures in futures contracts, this is also the immediate change in the wealth of the holder of the futures contract. The delta of the futures contract is therefore $e^{(r-q)T}$. We conclude that the deltas of a futures and forward contract are not the same. The delta of the futures is greater than the delta of the corresponding forward by a factor of e^{rT}.

118

Problem 17.22.

A bank's position in options on the dollar–euro exchange rate has a delta of 30,000 and a gamma of −80,000. Explain how these numbers can be interpreted. The exchange rate (dollars per euro) is 0.90. What position would you take to make the position delta neutral? After a short period of time, the exchange rate moves to 0.93. Estimate the new delta. What additional trade is necessary to keep the position delta neutral? Assuming the bank did set up a delta-neutral position originally, has it gained or lost money from the exchange-rate movement?

The delta indicates that when the value of the euro exchange rate increases by $0.01, the value of the bank's position increases by $0.01 \times 30{,}000 = \$300$. The gamma indicates that when the euro exchange rate increases by $0.01 the delta of the portfolio decreases by $0.01 \times 80{,}000 = 800$. For delta neutrality 30,000 euros should be shorted. When the exchange rate moves up to 0.93, we expect the delta of the portfolio to decrease by $(0.93 - 0.90) \times 80{,}000 = 2{,}400$ so that it becomes 27,600. To maintain delta neutrality, it is therefore necessary for the bank to unwind its short position 2,400 euros so that a net 27,600 have been shorted. As shown in the text (see Figure 17.8), when a portfolio is delta neutral and has a negative gamma, a loss is experienced when there is a large movement in the underlying asset price. We can conclude that the bank is likely to have lost money.

CHAPTER 18
Binomial Trees in Practice

This chapter provides more detail on the use of binomial trees than Chapter 12. It starts by explaining where the formulas for u, d and p come from. The formulas ensure that

1. The expected return on the stock in time Δt is the risk-free rate, r.

2. The standard deviation of the return in time Δt is $\sigma\sqrt{\Delta t}$ where σ is the volatility

Make sure you understand the calculations in Figure 18.3.

The chapter shows how the Greek letters discussed in Chapter 17 can be calculated. For delta we look at the two nodes at time Δt. We calculate the change in the option price when we move from the lower node to the upper node and the change in the stock price when we do so. Delta is the ratio of the option price change to the stock price change. Gamma is calculated from the three nodes at time $2\Delta t$. The upper two nodes produce one delta estimate and the lower two nodes produce another delta estimate. These two estimates of delta can be used to provide an estimate of gamma. Theta can be calculated from the tree by comparing option prices at time zero with the option price at the middle node at time $2\Delta t$. Vega is calculated by making a small change to the volatility, recomputing the tree, and observing the option value calculated.

An important issue for stock options is how to deal with dividends. On approach is to assume a known dividend yield (i.e., to assume that the dividend as a percent of the stock price is known). This is fairly straightforward. In many instances it is more accurate to assume the cash amount of the dividend is known. As indicated in Figure 18.6, the tree does not naturally recombine when this assumption is made. An approach that ensures a recombining tree is constructed in two stages:

1. Build a tree for the stock price less the present value of future dividends during the life of the option, and

2. Add the present value of future dividends at each node to construct the final tree

In Example 18.3, the first stage results in the tree in Figure 18.3. The second stage results in the tree attached to the Example.

Sections 18.4 and 18.5 discuss a number of extensions of the basic tree-building approach. They show that:

1. We can make the short-term interest rate a function of time by making the probability of an up movement a function of time

2. We can improve accuracy by using the same tree to value both an American option and the corresponding European option. The error in the price of the European option is assumed to be the same as that of the American option. (This is known as the control variate technique)

3. Instead of setting $d = 1/u$ we can choose the geometry of the tree so that $p = 0.5$. (See Section 18.5.)

120

Section 18.6 points out that instead of working back from the end of the tree to the beginning, we can use Monte Carlo simulation to sample paths starting at the beginning of the tree. Study the example in Section 18.6 to make sure you understand how to use this technique to price path-dependent options.

SOLUTIONS TO PRACTICE QUESTIONS

Problem 18.8.

Consider an option that pays off the amount by which the final stock price exceeds the average stock price achieved during the life of the option. Can this be valued from a binomial tree using backwards induction?

No! This is an example of a *path-dependent option*. The payoff depends on the path followed by the stock price as well as on its final value. The option cannot be valued by starting at the end of the tree and working backward, because the payoff at a final branch depends on the path used to reach it. European options for which the payoff depends on the average stock price can be valued using Monte Carlo simulation, as described in Section 18.6.

Problem 18.9.

A nine-month American put option on a non-dividend-paying stock has a strike price of $49. The stock price is $50, the risk-free rate is 5% per annum, and the volatility is 30% per annum. Use a three-step binomial tree to calculate the option price.

In this case, $S_0 = 50$, $K = 49$, $r = 0.05$, $\sigma = 0.30$, $T = 0.75$, and $\Delta t = 0.25$. Also

$$u = e^{\sigma\sqrt{\Delta t}} = e^{0.30\sqrt{0.25}} = 1.1618$$

$$d = \frac{1}{u} = 0.8607$$

$$a = e^{r\Delta t} = e^{0.05 \times 0.25} = 1.0126$$

$$p = \frac{a-d}{u-d} = 0.5043$$

$$1 - p = 0.4957$$

The output from DerivaGem for this example is shown in the Figure S18.1. The calculated price of the option is $4.29. Using 100 steps the price obtained is $3.91

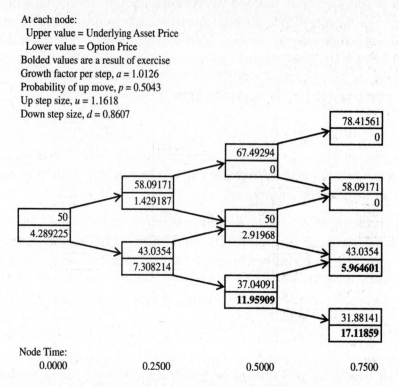

At each node:
  Upper value = Underlying Asset Price
  Lower value = Option Price
Bolded values are a result of exercise
Growth factor per step, $a = 1.0126$
Probability of up move, $p = 0.5043$
Up step size, $u = 1.1618$
Down step size, $d = 0.8607$

Node Time:
0.0000   0.2500   0.5000   0.7500

Figure S18.1   Tree for Problem 18.9

Problem 18.10.

Use a three-time-step tree to value a nine-month American call option on wheat futures. The current futures price is 400 cents, the strike price is 420 cents, the risk-free rate is 6%, and the volatility is 35% per annum. Estimate the delta of the option from your tree.

In this case $F_0 = 400$, $K = 420$, $r = 0.06$, $\sigma = 0.35$, $T = 0.75$, and $\Delta t = 0.25$. Also

$$u = e^{0.35\sqrt{0.25}} = 1.1912$$

$$d = \frac{1}{u} = 0.8395$$

$$a = 1$$

$$p = \frac{a - d}{u - d} = 0.4564$$

$$1 - p = 0.5436$$

The output from DerivaGem for this example is shown in the Figure S18.2. The calculated price of the option is 42.07 cents. Using 100 time steps the price obtained is 38.64. The option's delta is calculated from the tree is

$$(79.971 - 11.419)/(476.498 - 335.783) = 0.487$$

When 100 steps are used the estimate of the option's delta is 0.483.

122

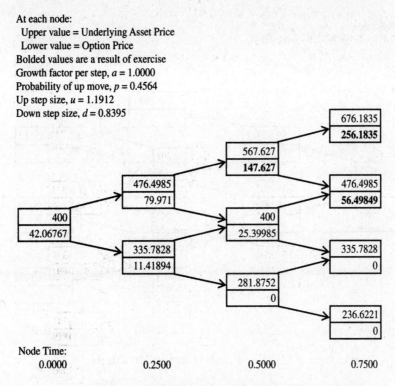

At each node:
  Upper value = Underlying Asset Price
  Lower value = Option Price
Bolded values are a result of exercise
Growth factor per step, $a = 1.0000$
Probability of up move, $p = 0.4564$
Up step size, $u = 1.1912$
Down step size, $d = 0.8395$

Node Time:
0.0000   0.2500   0.5000   0.7500

Figure S18.2   Tree for Problem 18.10

Problem 18.11.

A three-month American call option on a stock has a strike price of $20. The stock price is $20, the risk-free rate is 3% per annum, and the volatility is 25% per annum. A dividend of $2 is expected in 1.5 months. Use a three-step binomial tree to calculate the option price.

In this case the present value of the dividend is $2e^{-0.03 \times 0.125} = 1.9925$. We first build a tree for $S_0 = 20 - 1.9925 = 18.0075$, $K = 20$, $r = 0.03$, $\sigma = 0.25$, and $T = 0.25$ with $\Delta t = 0.08333$. This gives Figure S18.3. For nodes between times 0 and 1.5 months we then add the present value of the dividend to the stock price. The result is the tree in Figure S18.4. The price of the option calculated from the tree is 0.674. When 100 steps are used the price obtained is 0.690.

Tree shows stock prices less PV of dividend at 0.125 years
Growth factor per step, $a = 1.0025$
Probability of up move, $p = 0.49933$
Up step size, $u = 1.0748$
Down step size, $d = 0.9304$

| | | | 22.36047 |

| | | 20.8036 | |

| | 19.35512 | | 19.35512 |

| 18.0075 | | 18.0075 | |

| | 16.75371 | | 16.75371 |

| | | 15.58721 | |

| | | | 14.50193 |

Node Time:
0.0000   0.0833   0.1667   0.2500

Figure S18.3   First tree for Problem 18.11

At each node:
  Upper value = Underlying Asset Price
  Lower value = Option Price
Bolded values are a result of exercise
Probability of up move, $p = 0.4993$

| | | | 22.36045 **2.360453** |

| | | 20.80358 1.175614 | |

| | 21.35261 **1.352609** | | 19.35511 0 |

| 20 0.673662 | | 18.00749 0 | |

| | 18.7512 0 | | 16.75369 0 |

| | | 15.5872 0 | |

| | | | 14.50192 0 |

Node Time:
0.0000   0.0833   0.1667   0.2500

Figure S18.4   Final Tree for Problem 18.11

Problem 18.12.

A one-year American put option on a non-dividend-paying stock has an exercise price of $18. The current stock price is $20, the risk-free interest rate is 15% per annum, and the volatility of the stock is 40% per annum. Use the DerivaGem software with four three-

month time steps to estimate the value of the option. Display the tree and verify that the option prices at the final and penultimate nodes are correct. Use DerivaGem to value the European version of the option. Use the control variate technique to improve your estimate of the price of the American option.

In this case $S_0 = 20$, $K = 18$, $r = 0.15$, $\sigma = 0.40$, $T = 1$, and $\Delta t = 0.25$. The parameters for the tree are

$$u = e^{\sigma\sqrt{\Delta t}} = e^{0.4\sqrt{0.25}} = 1.2214$$

$$d = 1/u = 0.8187$$

$$a = e^{r\Delta t} = 1.0382$$

$$p = \frac{a - d}{u - d} = \frac{1.0382 - 0.8187}{1.2214 - 0.8187} = 0.545$$

The tree produced by DerivaGem for the American option is shown in Figure S18.5. The estimated value of the American option is \$1.29.

As shown in Figure S18.6, the same tree can be used to value a European put option with the same parameters. The estimated value of the European option is \$1.14. The option parameters are $S_0 = 20$, $K = 18$, $r = 0.15$, $\sigma = 0.40$ and $T = 1$

$$d_1 = \frac{\ln(20/18) + 0.15 + 0.40^2/2}{0.40} = 0.8384$$

$$d_2 = d_1 - 0.40 = 0.4384$$

$$N(-d_1) = 0.2009; \quad N(-d_2) = 0.3306$$

The true European put price is therefore

$$18e^{-0.15} \times 0.3306 - 20 \times 0.2009 = 1.10$$

This can also be obtained from DerivaGem. The control variate estimate of the American put price is therefore $1.29 + 1.10 - 1.14 = \$1.25$.

Problem 18.13.

A two-month American put option on a stock index has an exercise price of 480. The current level of the index is 484, the risk-free interest rate is 10% per annum, the dividend yield on the index is 3% per annum, and the volatility of the index is 25% per annum. Divide the life of the option into four half-month periods and use the binomial tree approach to estimate the value of the option.

In this case $S_0 = 484$, $K = 480$, $r = 0.10$, $\sigma = 0.25$ $q = 0.03$, $T = 0.1667$, and $\Delta t = 0.04167$

$$u = e^{\sigma\sqrt{\Delta t}} = e^{0.25\sqrt{0.04167}} = 1.0524$$

$$d = \frac{1}{u} = 0.9502$$

$$a = e^{(r-q)\Delta t} = 1.00292$$

$$p = \frac{a - d}{u - d} = \frac{1.0029 - 0.9502}{1.0524 - 0.9502} = 0.516$$

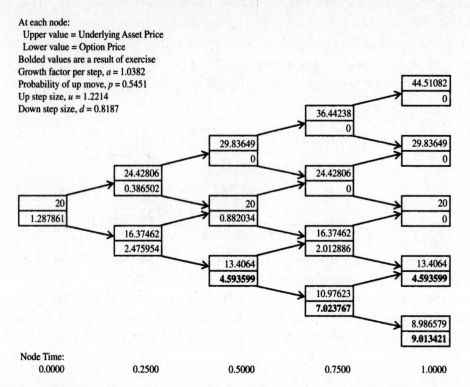

At each node:
  Upper value = Underlying Asset Price
  Lower value = Option Price
Bolded values are a result of exercise
Growth factor per step, $a = 1.0382$
Probability of up move, $p = 0.5451$
Up step size, $u = 1.2214$
Down step size, $d = 0.8187$

| | 44.51082 |
| | 0 |

| 36.44238 |
| 0 |

| 29.83649 | | 29.83649 |
| 0 | | 0 |

| 24.42806 | | 24.42806 |
| 0.386502 | | 0 |

| 20 | | 20 | | 20 |
| 1.287861 | | 0.882034 | | 0 |

| 16.37462 | | 16.37462 |
| 2.475954 | | 2.012886 |

| 13.4064 | | 13.4064 |
| **4.593599** | | **4.593599** |

| 10.97623 |
| **7.023767** |

| | 8.986579 |
| | **9.013421** |

Node Time:
0.0000   0.2500   0.5000   0.7500   1.0000

Figure S18.5   Tree to evaluate American option for Problem 18.12

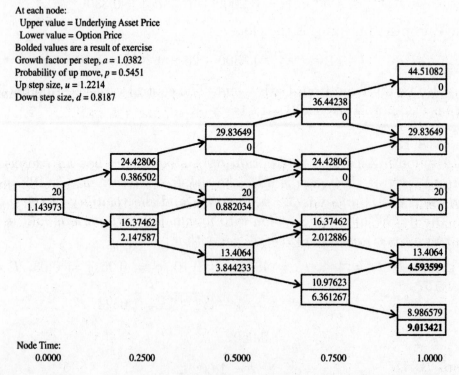

At each node:
  Upper value = Underlying Asset Price
  Lower value = Option Price
Bolded values are a result of exercise
Growth factor per step, $a = 1.0382$
Probability of up move, $p = 0.5451$
Up step size, $u = 1.2214$
Down step size, $d = 0.8187$

| | 44.51082 |
| | 0 |

| 36.44238 |
| 0 |

| 29.83649 | | 29.83649 |
| 0 | | 0 |

| 24.42806 | | 24.42806 |
| 0.386502 | | 0 |

| 20 | | 20 | | 20 |
| 1.143973 | | 0.882034 | | 0 |

| 16.37462 | | 16.37462 |
| 2.147587 | | 2.012886 |

| 13.4064 | | 13.4064 |
| 3.844233 | | **4.593599** |

| 10.97623 |
| 6.361267 |

| | 8.986579 |
| | **9.013421** |

Node Time:
0.0000   0.2500   0.5000   0.7500   1.0000

Figure S18.6   Tree to evaluate European option in Problem 18.12

126

The tree produced by DerivaGem is shown in the Figure S18.7. The estimated price of the option is $14.93.

At each node:
  Upper value = Underlying Asset Price
  Lower value = Option Price
Bolded values are a result of exercise
Growth factor per step, $a = 1.0029$
Probability of up move, $p = 0.5159$
Up step size, $u = 1.0524$
Down step size, $d = 0.9502$

				593.602 / 0
			564.0698 / 0	
		536.0069 / 0		536.0069 / 0
	509.3401 / 4.814811		509.3401 / 0	
484 / 14.93323		484 / 9.986432		484 / 0
	459.9206 / 25.84303		459.9206 / 20.71293	
		437.0392 / **42.96083**		437.0392 / **42.96083**
			415.2961 / **64.70388**	
				394.6348 / **85.36521**

Node Time:
0.0000   0.0417   0.0833   0.1250   0.1667

Figure S18.7   Tree to evaluate option in Problem 18.13

Problem 18.14.

How would you use the control variate approach to improve the estimate of the delta of an American option when the binomial tree approach is used?

First the delta of the American option is estimated in the usual way from the tree. Denote this by Δ_A^*. Then the delta of a European option which has the same parameters as the American option is calculated in the same way using the same tree. Denote this by Δ_B^*. Finally the true European delta, Δ_B, is calculated using the formulas in Chapter 17. The control variate estimate of delta is then:

$$\Delta_A^* - \Delta_B^* + \Delta_B$$

Problem 18.15.

How would you use the binomial tree approach to value an American option on a stock index when the dividend yield on the index is a function of time?

When the dividend yield is constant

$$u = e^{\sigma\sqrt{\Delta t}}$$

$$d = \frac{1}{u}$$

$$p = \frac{a - d}{u - d}$$

$$a = e^{(r-q)\Delta t}$$

Making the dividend yield, q, a function of time makes a, and therefore p, a function of time. However, it does not affect u or d. It follows that if q is a function of time we can use the same tree by making the probabilities a function of time. The interest rate r can also be a function of time as described in Section 18.4.

CHAPTER 19
Volatility Smiles

The Black–Scholes–Merton model and binomial trees assume that the probability distribution of the underlying asset at a future time is lognormal. If traders wanted to make that assumption they would use the same volatility to price options with different strike prices. In practice the implied volatility of an option is a function of the strike price. Figure 19.1 shows the typical situation for options on a foreign currency (The relationship between implied volatility and strike price is U-shaped). Figure 19.2 shows the future probability distribution for an exchange rate that is consistent with the implied volatilities that traders are using for foreign currency options. It has heavier right and left tails than the lognormal distribution. Figure 19.3 shows the typical situation for options on stocks and stock indices. (The implied volatility is a declining function of strike price.) Figure 19.4 shows the future probability distribution that is consistent with the implied volatilities that traders are using for stocks and stock indices. It has a heavier left tail and a less heavy right tail than the lognormal distribution.

Note that we do not have to worry about whether we are talking about put or call options when constructing diagrams such as Figure 19.1 and 19.3. This is because put–call parity shows that the implied volatility of a European put should be the same as that of a European call. (See Appendix to Chapter 19.) The same is usually approximately true of American options.

The volatility smile for options on foreign currencies in Figure 19.1 is likely a result of jumps and the fact that volatility is not constant. The volatility smile for options on equity in Figure 19.3 can be explained by the impact of leverage. (As the stock price declines the company becomes more highly levered and volatility increases.) Another explanation is crashophobia. (Since 1987 traders have been very concerned about the possibility of another stock market crash and have as a result increased the prices of deep-out-of-the-money put options.)

The Black–Scholes–Merton and similar models are in practice used to communicate the prices of European and American call and put options. Traders use a volatility surface such a that shown in Table 19.2 when trading options. The volatility surface enables them to estimate the appropriate implied volatility for any standard option trade that is proposed.

SOLUTIONS TO PRACTICE QUESTIONS

Problem 19.8.

A stock price is currently $20. Tomorrow, news is expected to be announced that will either increase the price by $5 or decrease the price by $5. What are the problems in using Black–Scholes to value one-month options on the stock?

The probability distribution of the stock price in one month is not lognormal. Possibly it consists of two lognormal distributions superimposed upon each other and is bimodal.

Black–Scholes is clearly inappropriate, because it assumes that the stock price at any future time is lognormal.

Problem 19.9.

What volatility smile is likely to be observed for six-month options when the volatility is uncertain and positively correlated to the stock price?

When the asset price is positively correlated with volatility, the volatility tends to increase as the asset price increases, producing less heavy left tails and heavier right tails. Implied volatility then increases with the strike price.

Problem 19.10.

What problems do you think would be encountered in testing a stock option pricing model empirically?

There are a number of problems in testing an option pricing model empirically. These include the problem of obtaining synchronous data on stock prices and option prices, the problem of estimating the dividends that will be paid on the stock during the option's life, the problem of distinguishing between situations where the market is inefficient and situations where the option pricing model is incorrect, and the problems of estimating stock price volatility.

Problem 19.11.

Suppose that a central bank's policy is to allow an exchange rate to fluctuate between 0.97 and 1.03. What pattern of implied volatilities for options on the exchange rate would you expect to see?

In this case the probability distribution of the exchange rate has a thin left tail and a thin right tail relative to the lognormal distribution. We are in the opposite situation to that described for foreign currencies in Section 19.1. Both out-of-the-money and in-the-money calls and puts can be expected to have lower implied volatilities than at-the-money calls and puts. The pattern of implied volatilities is likely to be similar to Figure 19.7.

Problem 19.12.

Option traders sometimes refer to deep-out-of-the-money options as being options on volatility. Why do you think they do this?

A deep-out-of-the-money option has a low value. Decreases in its volatility reduce its value. However, this reduction is small because the value can never go below zero. Increases in its volatility, on the other hand, can lead to significant percentage increases in the value of the option. The option does, therefore, have some of the same attributes as an option on volatility.

Problem 19.13.

A European call option on a certain stock has a strike price of $30, a time to maturity of one year, and an implied volatility of 30%. A European put option on the same stock has a strike price of $30, a time to maturity of one year, and an implied volatility of 33%.

130

What is the arbitrage opportunity open to a trader? Does the arbitrage work only when the lognormal assumption underlying Black–Scholes–Merton holds? Explain the reasons for your answer carefully.

As explained in the appendix to the chapter, put–call parity implies that European put and call options have the same implied volatility. If a call option has an implied volatility of 30% and a put option has an implied volatility of 33%, the call is priced too low relative to the put. The correct trading strategy is to buy the call, sell the put and short the stock. This does not depend on the lognormal assumption underlying Black–Scholes–Merton. Put–call parity is true for any set of assumptions.

Problem 19.14.

Suppose that the result of a major lawsuit affecting a company is due to be announced tomorrow. The company's stock price is currently $60. If the ruling is favorable to the company, the stock price is expected to jump to $75. If it is unfavorable, the stock is expected to jump to $50. What is the risk-neutral probability of a favorable ruling? Assume that the volatility of the company's stock will be 25% for six months after the ruling if the ruling is favorable and 40% if it is unfavorable. Use DerivaGem to calculate the relationship between implied volatility and strike price for six-month European options on the company today. The company does not pay dividends. Assume that the six-month risk-free rate is 6%. Consider call options with strike prices of $30, $40, $50, $60, $70, and $80.

Suppose that p is the probability of a favorable ruling. The expected price of the company's stock tomorrow is

$$75p + 50(1 - p) = 50 + 25p$$

This must be the price of the stock today. (We ignore the expected return to an investor over one day.) Hence

$$50 + 25p = 60$$

or $p = 0.4$.

If the ruling is favorable, the volatility, σ, will be 25%. Other option parameters are $S_0 = 75$, $r = 0.06$, and $T = 0.5$. For a value of K equal to 50, DerivaGem gives the value of a European call option price as 26.502.

If the ruling is unfavorable, the volatility, σ will be 40% Other option parameters are $S_0 = 50$, $r = 0.06$, and $T = 0.5$. For a value of K equal to 50, DerivaGem gives the value of a European call option price as 6.310.

The value today of a European call option with a strike price today is the weighted average of 26.502 and 6.310 or:

$$0.4 \times 26.502 + 0.6 \times 6.310 = 14.387$$

DerivaGem can be used to calculate the implied volatility when the option has this price. The parameter values are $S_0 = 60$, $K = 50$, $T = 0.5$, $r = 0.06$ and $c = 14.387$. The implied volatility is 47.76%.

These calculations can be repeated for other strike prices. The results are shown in the table below. The pattern of implied volatilities is shown in Figure S19.1.

Strike Price	Call Option Price Favorable Outcome	Call Option Price Unfavorable Outcome	Weighted Price	Implied Volatility (%)
30	45.887	21.001	30.955	46.67
40	36.182	12.437	21.935	47.78
50	26.502	6.310	14.387	47.76
60	17.171	2.826	8.564	46.05
70	9.334	1.161	4.430	43.22
80	4.159	0.451	1.934	40.36

Figure S19.1   Implied Volatilities in Problem 19.14

Problem 19.15.

An exchange rate is currently 0.8000. The volatility of the exchange rate is quoted as 12% and interest rates in the two countries are the same. Using the lognormal assumption, estimate the probability that the exchange rate in three months will be (a) less than 0.7000, (b) between 0.7000 and 0.7500, (c) between 0.7500 and 0.8000, (d) between 0.8000 and 0.8500, (e) between 0.8500 and 0.9000, and (f) greater than 0.9000. Based on the volatility smile usually observed in the market for exchange rates, which of these estimates would you expect to be too low and which would you expect to be too high?

132

As pointed out in Chapters 5 and 15 an exchange rate behaves like a stock that provides a dividend yield equal to the foreign risk-free rate. Whereas the growth rate in a non-dividend-paying stock in a risk-neutral world is r, the growth rate in the exchange rate in a risk-neutral world is $r - r_f$. Exchange rates have low systematic risks and so we can reasonably assume that this is also the growth rate in the real world. In this case the foreign risk-free rate equals the domestic risk-free rate ($r = r_f$). The expected growth rate in the exchange rate is therefore zero. If S_T is the exchange rate at time T its probability distribution is given by equation (12.2) with $\mu = 0$:

$$\ln S_T \sim \phi(\ln S_0 - \sigma^2 T/2, \sigma\sqrt{T})$$

where S_0 is the exchange rate at time zero and σ is the volatility of the exchange rate. In this case $S_0 = 0.8000$ and $\sigma = 0.12$, and $T = 0.25$ so that

$$\ln S_T \sim \phi(\ln 0.8 - 0.12^2 \times 0.25/2, 0.12\sqrt{0.25})$$

or

$$\ln S_T \sim \phi(-0.2249, 0.06)$$

(a) $\ln 0.70 = -0.3567$. The probability that $S_T < 0.70$ is the same as the probability that $\ln S_T < -0.3567$. It is

$$N\left(\frac{-0.3567 + 0.2249}{0.06}\right) = N(-2.1955)$$

This is 1.41%.

(b) $\ln 0.75 = -0.2877$. The probability that $S_T < 0.75$ is the same as the probability that $\ln S_T < -0.2877$. It is

$$N\left(\frac{-0.2877 + 0.2249}{0.06}\right) = N(-1.0456)$$

This is 14.79%. The probability that the exchange rate is between 0.70 and 0.75 is therefore $14.79 - 1.41 = 13.38\%$.

(c) $\ln 0.80 = -0.2231$. The probability that $S_T < 0.80$ is the same as the probability that $\ln S_T < -0.2231$. It is

$$N\left(\frac{-0.2231 + 0.2249}{0.06}\right) = N(0.0300)$$

This is 51.20%. The probability that the exchange rate is between 0.75 and 0.80 is therefore $51.20 - 14.79 = 36.41\%$.

(d) $\ln 0.85 = -0.1625$. The probability that $S_T < 0.85$ is the same as the probability that $\ln S_T < -0.1625$. It is

$$N\left(\frac{-0.1625 + 0.2249}{0.06}\right) = N(1.0404)$$

133

This is 85.09%. The probability that the exchange rate is between 0.80 and 0.85 is therefore $85.09 - 51.20 = 33.89\%$.

(e) $\ln 0.90 = -0.1054$. The probability that $S_T < 0.90$ is the same as the probability that $\ln S_T < -0.1054$. It is

$$N\left(\frac{-0.1054 + 0.2249}{0.06}\right) = N(1.9931)$$

This is 97.69%. The probability that the exchange rate is between 0.85 and 0.90 is therefore $97.69 - 85.09 = 12.60\%$.

(f) The probability that the exchange rate is greater than 0.90 is $100 - 97.69 = 2.31\%$

The volatility smile encountered for foreign exchange options is shown in Figure 19.1 of the text and implies the probability distribution in Figure 19.2. Figure 19.2 suggests that we would expect the probabilities in (a), (c), (d), and (f) to be too low and the probabilities in (b) and (e) to be too high.

Problem 19.16.

The price of a stock is $40. A six-month European call option on the stock with a strike price of $30 has an implied volatility of 35%. A six month European call option on the stock with a strike price of $50 has an implied volatility of 28%. The six-month risk-free rate is 5% and no dividends are expected. Explain why the two implied volatilities are different. Use DerivaGem to calculate the prices of the two options. Use put–call parity to calculate the prices of six-month European put options with strike prices of $30 and $50. Use DerivaGem to calculate the implied volatilities of these two put options.

The difference between the two implied volatilities is consistent with Figure 19.3 in the text. For equities the volatility smile is downward sloping. A high strike price option has a lower implied volatility than a low strike price option. The reason is that traders consider that the probability of a large downward movement in the stock price is higher than that predicted by the lognormal probability distribution. The implied distribution assumed by traders is shown in Figure 19.4.

To use DerivaGem to calculate the price of the first option, proceed as follows. Select Equity as the Underlying Type in the first worksheet. Select Analytic European as the Option Type. Input the stock price as 40, volatility as 35%, risk-free rate as 5%, time to exercise as 0.5 year, and exercise price as 30. Leave the dividend table blank because we are assuming no dividends. Select the button corresponding to call. Do not select the implied volatility button. Hit the *Enter* key and click on calculate. DerivaGem will show the price of the option as 11.155. Change the volatility to 28% and the strike price to 50. Hit the *Enter* key and click on calculate. DerivaGem will show the price of the option as 0.725.

Put–call parity is

$$c + Ke^{-rT} = p + S_0$$

so that

$$p = c + Ke^{-rT} - S_0$$

For the first option, $c = 11.155$, $S_0 = 40$, $r = 0.054$, $K = 30$, and $T = 0.5$ so that

$$p = 11.155 + 30e^{-0.05 \times 0.5} - 40 = 0.414$$

For the second option, $c = 0.725$, $S_0 = 40$, $r = 0.06$, $K = 50$, and $T = 0.5$ so that

$$p = 0.725 + 50e^{-0.05 \times 0.5} - 40 = 9.490$$

To use DerivaGem to calculate the implied volatility of the first put option, input the stock price as 40, the risk-free rate as 5%, time to exercise as 0.5 year, and the exercise price as 30. Input the price as 0.414 in the second half of the Option Data table. Select the buttons for a put option and implied volatility. Hit the *Enter* key and click on calculate. DerivaGem will show the implied volatility as 34.99%.

Similarly, to use DerivaGem to calculate the implied volatility of the first put option, input the stock price as 40, the risk-free rate as 5%, time to exercise as 0.5 year, and the exercise price as 50. Input the price as 9.490 in the second half of the Option Data table. Select the buttons for a put option and implied volatility. Hit the *Enter* key and click on calculate. DerivaGem will show the implied volatility as 27.99%.

These results are what we would expect. DerivaGem gives the implied volatility of a put with strike price 30 to be almost exactly the same as the implied volatility of a call with a strike price of 30. Similarly, it gives the implied volatility of a put with strike price 50 to be almost exactly the same as the implied volatility of a call with a strike price of 50.

Problem 19.17.

"The Black–Scholes–Merton model is used by traders as an interpolation tool." Discuss this view.

When plain vanilla call and put options are being priced, traders do use the Black–Scholes model as an interpolation tool. They calculate implied volatilities for the options whose prices they can observe in the market. By interpolating between strike prices and between times to maturity, they estimate implied volatilities for other options. These implied volatilities are then substituted into Black–Scholes to calculate prices for these options. In practice much of the work in producing a table such as Table 19.2 in the over-the-counter market is done by brokers. Brokers often act as intermediaries between participants in the over-the-counter market and usually have more information on the trades taking place than any individual financial institution. The brokers provide a table such as Table 19.2 to their clients as a service.

Problem 19.18

Using Table 19.2 calculate the implied volatility a trader would use for an 8-month option with a strike price of 1.04.

13.45%. We get the same answer by (a) interpolating between strike prices of 1.00 and 1.05 and then between maturities six months and one year and (b) interpolating between maturities of six months and one year and then between strike prices of 1.00 and 1.05.

CHAPTER 20
Value at Risk

Value at risk (VaR) has become a very important risk measure since the early 1990s. It is the loss on a portfolio that, with a certain confidence level, will not be exceeded. Suppose that the 10-day, 99% VaR is $5.6 million for a bank. This means that the probability of the bank's losses over the next 10 days being greater than $5.6 million is 1%. Bank regulators base the capital they require for market risk on a calculation of the 10-day, 99% VaR.

There are two ways of calculating VaR. The first is historical simulation. The second is the "model building" or "variance–covariance" approach. Historical simulation involves using the history of how market variables have behaved during the last N days to estimate a one-day VaR. It generates N scenarios. The first scenario assumes that the percentage change in all variables between today and tomorrow is the same as that between day 0 and day 1 of the historical data; the second scenario assumes that the percentage change in all variables between today and tomorrow is the same as that between day 1 and day 2 of the historical data; and so on. The scenarios are used to create a probability distribution for the change in the value of the current portfolio between today and tomorrow. This in turn allows the one-day value at risk to be determined. The 10-day value at risk is calculated as the one-day value at risk multiplied by $\sqrt{10}$.

The model building approach uses a model for the daily change in the values of market variables. Like the historical simulation approach its initial focus is on the one-day VaR. The most common assumption is that the changes have a multivariate normal distribution. If the change in the value of the portfolio is linearly related to the changes in the values of the variables, the one-day change in the value of the portfolio is normally distributed. The mean change is usually assumed to be zero. The standard deviation of the change can be calculated from the standard deviations of, and correlations between, the market variables. This enables the one-day value at risk to be calculated. As in the case of the historical simulation approach, the 10-day value at risk is assumed to be $\sqrt{10}$ times the one-day value at risk.

Options create problems for the model building approach. This is because the change in the value of an option is not linearly related to the change in the value of the underlying variables. One approach is to use the delta of the option to define an approximately linear relationship. However, this can lead to serious inaccuracies. Another approach is to use delta and gamma and assume a quadratic relationship between the change in the value of the option and changes in the values of the underlying market variables.

The model building approach requires estimates of volatilities and correlations for the market variables. (The volatility is the daily volatility and is defined as the standard deviation of percentage daily changes.) A popular estimation approach is the exponentially weighted moving average (EWMA) method. This applies weights to observations that decrease exponentially as we move back through time. The nice thing about the EWMA approach is that relatively little data needs to be kept. For example to update a volatility estimate all we need is the most recent change in the market variable. (See equation 20.10). Similarly to update an estimate of the correlation between two variables all we need are the most recent changes in the variables. (See equation 20.12) The updating is actually carried out in terms of variances and covariances. The variance is the square of the volatility. The covariance is the correlation multiplied by the product of the volatilities of the two variables.

SOLUTIONS TO PRACTICE QUESTIONS

Problem 20.8.

A company uses an EWMA model for forecasting volatility. It decides to change the parameter λ from 0.95 to 0.85. Explain the likely impact on the forecasts.

Reducing λ from 0.95 to 0.85 means that more weight is put on recent observations of u_i^2 and less weight is given to older observations. Volatilities calculated with $\lambda = 0.85$ will react more quickly to new information and will "bounce around" much more than volatilities calculated with $\lambda = 0.95$.

Problem 20.9.

Explain the difference between value at risk and expected shortfall.

Value at risk is the loss that is expected to be exceeded $(100 - X)\%$ of the time in N days for specified parameter values, X and N. Expected shortfall is the expected loss conditional that the loss is greater than the Value at Risk.

Problem 20.10.

Consider a position consisting of a $100,000 investment in asset A and a $100,000 investment in asset B. Assume that the daily volatilities of both assets are 1% and that the coefficient of correlation between their returns is 0.3. What is the 5-day 99% value at risk for the portfolio?

The standard deviation of the daily change in the investment in each asset is $1,000. The variance of the portfolio's daily change is

$$1,000^2 + 1,000^2 + 2 \times 0.3 \times 1,000 \times 1,000 = 2,600,000$$

The standard deviation of the portfolio's daily change is the square root of this or $1,612.45. The standard deviation of the 5-day change is

$$1,612.45 \times \sqrt{5} = \$3,605.55$$

From the tables of $N(x)$ we see that $N(-2.33) = 0.01$. This means that 1% of a normal distribution lies more than 2.33 standard deviations below the mean. The 5-day 99 percent value at risk is therefore $2.33 \times 3,605.55 = \$8,400.93$.

Problem 20.11.

The volatility of a certain market variable is 30% per annum. Calculate a 99% confidence interval for the size of the percentage daily change in the variable.

The volatility per day is $30/\sqrt{252} = 1.89\%$. There is a 99% chance that a normally distributed variable will lie within 2.57 standard deviations. We are therefore 99% confident that the daily change will be less than $2.57 \times 1.89 = 4.86\%$.

Problem 20.12.

Explain how an interest rate swap is mapped into a portfolio of zero-coupon bonds with standard maturities for the purposes of a VaR calculation.

When a final exchange of principal is added in, the floating side is equivalent a zero-coupon bond with a maturity date equal to the date of the next payment. The fixed side is a coupon-bearing bond, which is equivalent to a portfolio of zero-coupon bonds. The swap can therefore be mapped into long and short positions in zero-coupon bonds with maturity dates corresponding to the payment dates. Each of the zero-coupon bonds can then be mapped into positions in the adjacent standard-maturity zero-coupon bonds. One way of doing this is described in the Appendix to Chapter 20.

Problem 20.13.

Explain why the linear model can provide only approximate estimates of VaR for a portfolio containing options.

The change in the value of an option is not linearly related to the percentage change in the value of the underlying variable. The linear model assumes that the change in the value of a portfolio is linearly related to percentage changes in the underlying variables. It is therefore only an approximation for a portfolio containing options.

Problem 20.14.

Verify that the 0.3-year zero-coupon bond in the cash-flow mapping example in the Appendix at the end of this chapter is mapped into a $37,397 position in a three-month bond and a $11,793 position in a six-month bond.

The 0.3-year cash flow is mapped into a 3-month zero-coupon bond and a 6-month zero-coupon bond. The 0.25 and 0.50 year rates are 5.50 and 6.00 respectively. Linear interpolation gives the 0.30-year rate as 5.60%. The present value of $50,000 received at time 0.3 years is

$$\frac{50,000}{1.056^{0.30}} = 49,189.32$$

The volatility of 0.25-year and 0.50-year zero-coupon bonds are 0.06% and 0.10% per day respectively. The interpolated volatility of a 0.30-year zero-coupon bond is therefore 0.068% per day.

Assume that w of the value of the 0.30-year cash flow gets allocated to a 3-month zero-coupon bond and $1-w$ to a six-month zero coupon bond. To match variances we must have

$$0.00068^2 = 0.0006^2 w^2 + 0.001^2 (1-w)^2 + 2 \times 0.9 \times 0.0006 \times 0.001 w(1-w)$$

138

or

$$0.28w^2 - 0.92w + 0.5376 = 0$$

Using the formula for the solution to a quadratic equation

$$w = \frac{-0.92 + \sqrt{0.92^2 - 4 \times 0.28 \times 0.5376}}{2 \times 0.28} = 0.760259$$

this means that a value of $0.760259 \times 49,189.32 = \$37,397$ is allocated to the three-month bond and a value of $0.239741 \times 49,189.32 = \$11,793$ is allocated to the six-month bond. The 0.3-year cash flow is therefore equivalent to a position of \$37,397 in a 3-month zero-coupon bond and a position of \$11,793 in a 6-month zero-coupon bond. This is consistent with the results in the Appendix to Chapter 20.

Problem 20.15.

Suppose that the 5-year and 7-year rates are 6% and 7%, respectively (both expressed with annual compounding), the daily volatility of a 5-year zero-coupon bond is 0.5%, and the daily volatility of a 7-year zero-coupon bond is 0.58%. The correlation between daily returns on the two bonds is 0.6. Map a cash flow of \$1,000 received at time 6.5 years into a position in a 5-year bond and a position in a 7-year bond using the approach in the Appendix at the end of this chapter. What cash flows in 5 and 7 years are equivalent to the 6.5-year cash flow?

The 6.5-year cash flow is mapped into a 5-year zero-coupon bond and a 7-year zero-coupon bond. The 5-year and 7-year rates are 6% and 7% respectively. Linear interpolation gives the 6.5-year rate as 6.75%. The present value of \$1,000 received at time 6.5 years is

$$\frac{1,000}{1.0675^{6.5}} = 654.05$$

The volatility of 5-year and 7-year zero-coupon bonds are 0.50% and 0.58% per day respectively. The interpolated volatility of a 6.5-year zero-coupon bond is therefore 0.56% per day.

Assume that w of the value of the 6.5-year cash flow gets allocated to a 5-year zero-coupon bond and $1 - w$ to a 7-year zero coupon bond. To match variances we must have

$$.56^2 = .50^2 w^2 + .58^2 (1 - w)^2 + 2 \times 0.6 \times .50 \times .58 w(1 - w)$$

or

$$.2384 w^2 - .3248 w + .0228 = 0$$

Using the formula for the solution to a quadratic equation

$$w = \frac{.3248 - \sqrt{.3248^2 - 4 \times .2384 \times .0228}}{2 \times .2384} = 0.074243$$

this means that a value of $0.074243 \times 654.05 = \$48.56$ is allocated to the 5-year bond and a value of $0.925757 \times 654.05 = \$605.49$ is allocated to the 7-year bond. The 6.5-year cash flow is therefore equivalent to a position of $48.56 in a 5-year zero-coupon bond and a position of $605.49 in a 7-year zero-coupon bond.

The equivalent 5-year and 7-year cash flows are $48.56 \times 1.06^5 = 64.98$ and $605.49 \times 1.07^7 = 972.28$.

Problem 20.16.

Some time ago a company entered into a forward contract to buy £1 million for $1.5 million. The contract now has six months to maturity. The daily volatility of a six-month zero-coupon sterling bond (when its price is translated to dollars) is 0.06% and the daily volatility of a six-month zero-coupon dollar bond is 0.05%. The correlation between returns from the two bonds is 0.8. The current exchange rate is 1.53. Calculate the standard deviation of the change in the dollar value of the forward contract in one day. What is the 10-day 99% VaR? Assume that the six-month interest rate in both sterling and dollars is 5% per annum with continuous compounding.

The contract is a long position in a sterling bond combined with a short position in a dollar bond. The value of the sterling bond is $1.53e^{-0.05\times0.5}$ or $1.492 million. The value of the dollar bond is $1.5e^{-0.05\times0.5}$ or $1.463 million. The variance of the change in the value of the contract in one day is

$$1.492^2 \times 0.0006^2 + 1.463^2 \times 0.0005^2 - 2 \times 0.8 \times 1.492 \times 0.0006 \times 1.463 \times 0.0005$$

$$= 0.000000288$$

The standard deviation is therefore $0.000537 million. The 10-day 99% VaR is $0.000537 \times \sqrt{10} \times 2.33 = \$0.00396$ million.

Problem 20.17.

The most recent estimate of the daily volatility of the U.S. dollar–sterling exchange rate is 0.6%, and the exchange rate at 4 p.m. yesterday was 1.5000. The parameter λ in the EWMA model is 0.9. Suppose that the exchange rate at 4 p.m. today proves to be 1.4950. How would the estimate of the daily volatility be updated?

The daily return is $-0.005/1.5000 = -0.003333$. The current daily variance estimate is $0.006^2 = 0.000036$. The new daily variance estimate is

$$0.9 \times 0.000036 + 0.1 \times 0.003333^2 = 0.000033511$$

The new volatility is the square root of this. It is 0.00579 or 0.579%.

Problem 20.18.

Suppose that the daily volatilities of asset A and asset B calculated at close of trading yesterday are 1.6% and 2.5%, respectively. The prices of the assets at close of trading yesterday were $20 and $40, and the estimate of the coefficient of correlation between the returns on the two assets made at close of trading yesterday was 0.25. The parameter λ used in the EWMA model is 0.95.

(a) Calculate the current estimate of the covariance between the assets.

(b) On the assumption that the prices of the assets at close of trading today are $20.5 and $40.5, update the correlation estimate.

(a) The volatilities and correlation imply that the current estimate of the covariance is $0.25 \times 0.016 \times 0.025 = 0.0001$.

(b) If the prices of the assets at close of trading today are $20.5 and $40.5, the returns are $0.5/20 = 0.025$ and $0.5/40 = 0.0125$. The new covariance estimate is

$$0.95 \times 0.0001 + 0.05 \times 0.025 \times 0.0125 = 0.0001106$$

The new variance estimate for asset A is

$$0.95 \times 0.016^2 + 0.05 \times 0.025^2 = 0.00027445$$

so that the new volatility is 0.0166. The new variance estimate for asset B is

$$0.95 \times 0.025^2 + 0.05 \times 0.0125^2 = 0.000601562$$

so that the new volatility is 0.0245. The new correlation estimate is

$$\frac{0.0001106}{0.0166 \times 0.0245} = 0.272$$

Problem 20.19.

Suppose that the daily volatility of the FT-SE 100 stock index (measured in pounds sterling) is 1.8% and the daily volatility of the dollar/sterling exchange rate is 0.9%. Suppose further that the correlation between the FT-SE 100 and the dollar/sterling exchange rate is 0.4. What is the volatility of the FT-SE 100 when it is translated to U.S. dollars? Assume that the dollar/sterling exchange rate is expressed as the number of U.S. dollars per pound sterling. (Hint: When $Z = XY$, the percentage daily change in Z is approximately equal to the percentage daily change in X plus the percentage daily change in Y.)

The FT-SE expressed in dollars is XY where X is the FT-SE expressed in sterling and Y is the exchange rate (value of one pound in dollars). Define x_i as the proportional change in X on day i and y_i as the proportional change in Y on day i. The proportional change in XY is approximately $x_i + y_i$. The standard deviation of x_i is 0.018 and the standard deviation of y_i is 0.009. The correlation between the two is 0.4. The variance of $x_i + y_i$ is therefore

$$0.018^2 + 0.009^2 + 2 \times 0.018 \times 0.009 \times 0.4 = 0.0005346$$

so that the volatility of $x_i + y_i$ is 0.0231 or 2.31%. This is the volatility of the FT-SE expressed in dollars. Note that it is greater than the volatility of the FT-SE expressed in sterling. This is the impact of the positive correlation. When the FT-SE increases the value of sterling measured in dollars also tends to increase. This creates an even bigger increase in the value of FT-SE measured in dollars. Similarly for a decrease in the FT-SE.

Problem 20.20.

Suppose that in Problem 20.19 the correlation between the S&P 500 Index (measured in dollars) and the FT-SE 100 Index (measured in sterling) is 0.7, the correlation between the S&P 500 index (measured in dollars) and the dollar-sterling exchange rate is 0.3, and the daily volatility of the S&P 500 Index is 1.6%. What is the correlation between the S&P 500 Index (measured in dollars) and the FT-SE 100 Index when it is translated to dollars? (Hint: For three variables X, Y, and Z, the covariance between X + Y and Z equals the covariance between X and Z plus the covariance between Y and Z.)

Continuing with the notation in Problem 20.19, define z_i as the proportional change in the value of the S&P 500 on day i. The covariance between x_i and z_i is $0.7 \times 0.018 \times 0.016 = 0.0002016$. The covariance between y_i and z_i is $0.3 \times 0.009 \times 0.016 = 0.0000432$. The covariance between $x_i + y_i$ and z_i equals the covariance between x_i and z_i plus the covariance between y_i and z_i. It is

$$0.0002016 + 0.0000432 = 0.0002448$$

The correlation between $x_i + y_i$ and z_i is

$$\frac{0.0002448}{0.016 \times 0.0231} = 0.662$$

Problem 20.21.

The one-day 99% VaR is calculated for the four-index example in Section 20.2 as $247,571. Look at the underlying spreadsheets on the author's web site and calculate the a) the 95% one-day VaR and b) the 97% one-day VaR.

The 95% one-day VaR is the 25th worst loss. This is $168,612. The 97% one-day VaR is the 15th worst loss. This is $188,758.

Problem 20.22.

Use the spreadsheets on the author's web site to calculate the one-day 99% VaR, using the basic methodology in Section 20.2 if the four-index portfolio considered in Section 20.2 is equally divided between the four indices.

In the "Scenarios" worksheet the portfolio investments are changed to 2500 in cells L2:O2. The losses are then sorted from the largest to the smallest. The fifth worst loss is $258,355. This is the one-day 99% VaR.

Problem 20.23.

At the end of Section 20.6, the VaR for the four-index example was calculated using the model-building approach. How does the VaR calculated change if the investment is $2.5 million in each index? Carry out calculations when a) volatilities and correlations *are estimated using the equally weighted model and b) when they are estimated using the EWMA model with* $\lambda = 0.94$. *Use the spreadsheets on the author's web site.*

The alpha's (row 21 for equal weights and row 7 for EWMA) should be changed to 2,500. This changes the one-day 99% VaR to \$238,022 when volatilities and correlations are estimated using the equally weighted model and to \$510,459 when EWMA with is used.

Problem 20.24.

What is the effect of changing λ *from 0.94 to 0.97 in the EWMA calculations in the four-index example at the end of Section 20.6? Use the spreadsheets on the author's web site.*

The parameter λ is in cell N3 of the EWMA worksheet. Changing it to 0.97 changes the one-day 99% VaR from \$488,217 to \$404,661. This is because less weight is given to recent observations.

CHAPTER 21
Interest Rate Options

The chapter describes the most common interest rate options and the standard market models that are used to price them. The exchange-traded interest rate options that are most common are options on interest rate futures (for example, options on Eurodollar futures and options on Treasury bond futures). They can be valued using the approach in Chapter 16. The commonest over-the-counter products are European bond options, interest rate caps, and European swap options.

European options on bonds are traded in the over-the-counter market. Typically an implied yield volatility is quoted. This yield volatility is converted into a price volatility (see equation 21.6) using an approximate duration result and the price volatility is used in a Black–Scholes type of formula where the bond price at the maturity of the option is assumed to be lognormal.

An interest-rate cap is an instrument that provides insurance against the rate paid on a floating rate loan going above a certain level. The level (known as the cap rate) is analogous to the strike price in a regular option. The rate on the floating rate loan is reset every month, every quarter, every six months, or every year. An interest rate cap therefore consists of a series of call options on future interest rates, one corresponding to each time the floating rate is reset. The individual options are referred to as caplets. Each caplet is valued using a Black–Scholes type of formula where the future interest rate is assumed to be lognormally distributed. (See equation 21.8.)

For any call option there is a corresponding put option. Interest rate caps are no exception. Just as an interest rate cap is a series of call options on interest rates, an interest rate floor is a series of put options on interest rates. As shown in Business Snapshot 21.1 there is a relationship between the values of an interest rate floor, an interest rate cap, and a swap. This is similar to the put–call parity relationship for regular call and put options.

A European swap option (often called a European swaption) is an option to enter into a swap at a particular future time. In the swap a fixed rate is exchanged for LIBOR. The fixed rate is analogous to the strike price in a regular option and is specified at the time the swap option is entered into. A swaption where the holder has the right to pay fixed and receive floating can be viewed as a call option on the swap rate (or as a put option on a par yield bond). A swaption where the holder has the right to receive fixed and pay floating can be viewed as a put option on the swap rate (or a call option on a par yield bond). A European swaption is valued by assuming that the swap rate at the maturity of the swap option is lognormally distributed. (See equations 21.10 and 21.11.)

SOLUTIONS TO PRACTICE QUESTIONS

Problem 21.8.

A bank uses Black's model to price European bond options. Suppose that an implied price volatility for a 5-year option on a bond maturing in 10 years is used to price a 9-year option on the bond. *Would you expect the resultant price to be too high or too low? Explain your answer.*

A one-year forward bond price has a lower volatility than a five-year forward bond price. The volatility used to price a nine-year option on a ten-year bond should therefore be less than that used to price a five-year option on a ten-year bond. Using the volatility backed out from the five-year option to price the nine-year option is therefore likely to produce a price that is too high.

Problem 21.9.

Consider a four-year European call option on a bond that will mature in five years. The five-year bond price is $105, the price of a four-year bond with the same coupon as the five-year bond is $102, the strike price of the option is $100, the four-year risk-free interest rate is 10% per annum (continuously compounded), and the volatility of the forward price of the bond underlying the option is 2% per annum. What is the present value of the principal in the four-year bond? What is the present value of the coupons in the four-year bond? What is the forward price of the bond underlying the option? What is the value of the option?

The present value of the principal in the four year bond is $100e^{-4\times0.1} = 67.032$. The present value of the coupons is, therefore, $102 - 67.032 = 34.968$. The coupons on the four-year bond are the income on the five-year bond during the life of the option. This means that the forward price of the bond underlying the option is

$$(105 - 34.968)e^{0.1\times4} = 104.475$$

The parameters in Black's model are therefore $F_0 = 104.475$, $K = 100$, $r = 0.1$, $T = 4$, and $\sigma = 0.02$.

$$d_1 = \frac{\ln 1.04475 + 0.5 \times 0.02^2 \times 4}{0.02\sqrt{4}} = 1.1144$$

$$d_2 = d_1 - 0.02\sqrt{4} = 1.0744$$

The price of the European call is

$$e^{-0.1\times4}[104.475N(1.1144) - 100N(1.0744)] = 3.19$$

or $3.19.

Problem 21.10.

If the yield volatility for a five-year put option on a bond maturing in 10 years time is specified as 22%, how should the option be valued? Assume that, based on today's interest rates the modified duration of the bond at the maturity of the option will be 4.2 years and the forward yield on the bond is 7%.

The relationship between the yield volatility and the price volatility is given by equation (21.6). In this case, the price volatility is

$$0.07 \times 4.2 \times 0.22 = 6.47\%$$

This is the volatility substituted into equation (21.2).

Problem 21.11.

A corporation knows that in three months it will have $5 million to invest for 90 days at LIBOR minus 50 basis points and wishes to ensure that the rate obtained will be at least 6.5%. What position in exchange-traded interest-rate options should the corporation take?

The rate received will be less than 6.5% when LIBOR is less than 7%. The corporation requires a three-month call option on a Eurodollar futures option with a strike price of 93. If three-month LIBOR is greater than 7% at the option maturity, the Eurodollar futures quote at option maturity will be less than 93 and there will be no payoff from the option. If the three-month LIBOR is less than 7%, one Eurodollar futures options provide a payoff of $25 per 0.01%. Each 0.01% of interest costs the corporation $500 (= 5,000,000 × 0.0001). A total of 500/25 = 20 contracts are therefore required.

Problem 21.12.

Explain carefully how you would use (a) spot volatilities and (b) flat volatilities to value a five-year cap.

When spot volatilities are used to value a cap, a different volatility is used to value each caplet. When flat volatilities are used, the same volatility is used to value each caplet within a given cap. Spot volatilities are a function of the maturity of the caplet. Flat volatilities are a function of the maturity of the cap.

Problem 21.13.

What other instrument is the same as a five-year zero-cost collar in which the strike price of the cap equals the strike price of the floor? What does the common strike price equal?

A 5-year zero-cost collar where the strike price of the cap equals the strike price of the floor is the same as an interest rate swap agreement to receive floating and pay a fixed rate equal to the strike price. The common strike price is the swap rate. Note that the swap is actually a forward swap that excludes the first exchange of payments. (See Business Snapshot 21.1.)

Problem 21.14.

Suppose that the 1-year, 2-year, 3-year, 4-year and 5-year zero rates are 6%, 6.4%, 6.7%, 6.9%, and 7%. The price of a 5-year semiannual cap with a principal of $100 at a cap rate of 8% is $3. Use DerivaGem to determine
  a. *The 5-year flat volatility for caps and floors*
  b. *The floor rate in a zero-cost 5-year collar when the cap rate is 8%*

We choose the Caps and Swap Options worksheet of DerivaGem and choose Cap/Floor as the Underlying Type. We enter the 1-, 2-, 3-, 4-, 5-year zero rates as 6%, 6.4%, 6.7%, 6.9%, and 7.0% in the Term Structure table. We enter Semiannual for the Settlement Frequency, 100 for the Principal, 0 for the Start (Years), 5 for the End (Years), 8% for the

Cap/Floor Rate, and $3 for the Price. We select Black-European as the Pricing Model and choose the Cap button. We check the Imply Volatility box and Calculate. The implied volatility is 24.79%. We then uncheck Implied Volatility, select Floor, check Imply Breakeven Rate. The floor rate that is calculated is 6.71%. This is the floor rate for which the floor is worth $3. A collar when the floor rate is 6.71% and the cap rate is 8% has zero cost.

Problem 21.15.

Show that $V_1 + f = V_2$ where V_1 is the value of a swaption to pay a fixed rate of R_K and receive LIBOR between times T_1 and T_2, f is the value of a forward swap to receive a fixed rate of R_K and pay LIBOR between times T_1 and T_2, and V_2 is the value of a swaption to receive a fixed rate of R_K between times T_1 and T_2. Deduce that $V_1 = V_2$ when R_K equals the current forward swap rate.

We prove this result by considering two portfolios. The first consists of the swap option to receive R_K; the second consists of the swap option to pay R_K and the forward swap. Suppose that the actual swap rate at the maturity of the options is greater than R_K. The swap option to pay R_K will be exercised and the swap option to receive R_K will not be exercised. Both portfolios are then worth zero since the swap option to pay R_K is neutralized by the forward swap. Suppose next that the actual swap rate at the maturity of the options is less than R_K. The swap option to receive R_K is exercised and the swap option to pay R_K is not exercised. Both portfolios are then equivalent to a swap where R_K is received and floating is paid. In all states of the world the two portfolios are worth the same at time T_1. They must therefore be worth the same today. This proves the result. When R_K equals the current forward swap rate $f = 0$ and $V_1 = V_2$. A swap option to pay fixed is therefore worth the same as a similar swap option to receive fixed when the fixed rate in the swap option is the forward swap rate.

Problem 21.16.

Explain why there is an arbitrage opportunity if the implied Black (flat) volatility for a cap is different from that for a floor. Do the broker quotes in Table 21.1 present an arbitrage opportunity?

The put–call parity relationship in Business Snapshot 21.2 is

$$\text{cap} + \text{swap} = \text{floor}$$

must hold for market prices. It also holds for Black's model. An argument similar to that in the appendix to Chapter 19 shows that the implied volatility of the cap must equal the implied volatility of the call. If this is not the case there is an arbitrage opportunity. The broker quotes in Table 21.1 do not present an arbitrage opportunity because the cap offer is always higher than the floor bid and the floor offer is always higher than the cap bid.

Problem 21.17.

Suppose that zero rates are as in Problem 21.14. Use DerivaGem to determine the value of an option to pay a fixed rate of 6% and receive LIBOR on a five-year swap *starting in one year. Assume that the principal is $100 million, payments are exchanged semiannually, and the swap rate volatility is 21%.*

We choose the Caps and Swap Options worksheet of DerivaGem and choose Swap Option as the Underlying Type. We enter 100 as the Principal, 1 as the Start (Years), 6 as the End (Years), 6% as the Swap Rate, and Semiannual as the Settlement Frequency. We choose Black-European as the pricing model, enter 21% as the Volatility and check the Pay Fixed button. We do not check the Imply Breakeven Rate and Imply Volatility boxes. The value of the swap option is 5.63.

CHAPTER 22
Exotic Options and Other Nonstandard Products

Derivatives traders have been very imaginative in designing new derivative instruments. This chapter attempts to give the reader a flavor for the nonstandard products that exist. It introduces exotic options, mortgage-backed securities, and non-standard swaps. Some of the instruments covered are designed to meet the hedging needs of corporate treasurers or fund managers; some are designed for tax, accounting, legal or regulatory reasons; some are simply interesting alternatives to the "plain vanilla" products.

The exotic options discussed include Bermudan options, forward start options, compound options, chooser options, barrier options, binary options, lookback options, shout options, and Asian options. You should make sure you understand how each of these work.

Agency mortgage-backed securities (MBSs) are important instruments in the United States. They are created when a financial institution securitizes part of its residential mortgage portfolio. The mortgages are put in a pool and investors acquire a stake in the pool by buying units. The mortgages are guaranteed against defaults by a government agency, but there is prepayment risk. As rates decline there is a tendency for mortgage holders to prepay. The prepayments are passed on to the MBS holders who then have to reinvest the funds at a lower rate of interest than they were earning before. Often mortgage-backed securities are designed so that different investors bear different amounts of prepayment risk.

The final part of the chapter discusses non-standard swaps. These are variations on the swaps discussed in Chapter 7. Among the different types of swaps discussed are those where the principal changes through time, where the floating interest rate is not LIBOR, where interest is compounded forward rather than being paid out, LIBOR-in-arrears swaps, CMS and CMT swaps, differential swaps, equity swaps, accrual swaps, cancelable swaps, index amortizing swaps, commodity swaps and volatility swaps. You should make sure you understand how they work.

SOLUTIONS TO PRACTICE QUESTIONS

Problem 22.8.
Describe the payoff from a portfolio consisting of a lookback call and a lookback put with the same maturity.

A lookback call provides a payoff of $S_T - S_{\min}$. A lookback put provides a payoff of $S_{\max} - S_T$. A combination of a lookback call and a lookback put therefore provides a payoff of $S_{\max} - S_{\min}$.

Problem 22.9.
Consider a chooser option where the holder has the right to choose between a European call and a European put at any time during a two-year period. The maturity dates and

strike prices for the calls and puts are the same regardless of when the choice is made. Is it ever optimal to make the choice before the end of the two-year period? Explain your answer.

No, it is never optimal to choose early. The resulting cash flows are the same regardless of when the choice is made. There is no point in the holder making a commitment earlier than necessary. This argument also applies when the holder chooses between two American options providing the options cannot be exercised before the two-year point. If the early exercise period starts as soon as the choice is made, the argument does not hold. For example, if the stock price fell to almost nothing in the first six months, the holder would choose a put option at this time and exercise it immediately.

Problem 22.10.

Suppose that c_1 and p_1 are the prices of a European average price call and a European average price put with strike price K and maturity T, c_2 and p_2 are the prices of a European average strike call and European average strike put with maturity T, and c_3 and p_3 are the prices of a regular European call and a regular European put with strike price K and maturity T. Show that

$$c_1 + c_2 - c_3 = p_1 + p_2 - p_3$$

The payoffs are as follows:
$c_1 : \max(S_{\text{ave}} - K, 0)$
$c_2 : \max(S_T - S_{\text{ave}}, 0)$
$c_3 : \max(S_T - K, 0)$
$p_1 : \max(K - S_{\text{ave}}, 0)$
$p_2 : \max(S_{\text{ave}} - S_T, 0)$
$p_3 : \max(K - S_T, 0)$
The payoff from $c_1 - p_1$ is always $S_{\text{ave}} - K$; The payoff from $c_2 - p_2$ is always $S_T - S_{\text{ave}}$; The payoff from $c_3 - p_3$ is always $S_T - K$; It follows that

$$c_1 - p_1 + c_2 - p_2 = c_3 - p_3$$

or

$$c_1 + c_2 - c_3 = p_1 + p_2 - p_3$$

Problem 22.11.

The text derives a decomposition of a particular type of chooser option into a call maturing at time T_2 and a put maturing at time T_1. By using put–call parity to obtain an expression for c instead of p, derive an alternative decomposition into a call maturing at time T_1 and a put maturing at time T_2.

Substituting for c, put-call parity gives

$$\max(c, p) = \max\left[p, p + S_1 e^{-q(T_2 - T_1)} - K e^{-r(T_2 - T_1)} \right]$$

$$= p + \max \left[0, S_1 e^{-q(T_2 - T_1)} - K e^{-r(T_2 - T_1)} \right]$$

$$= p + e^{-q(T_2 - T_1)} \max \left[0, S_1 - K e^{-(r-q)(T_2 - T_1)} \right]$$

This shows that the chooser option can be decomposed into

1. A put option with strike price K and maturity T_2; and
2. $e^{-q(T_2 - T_1)}$ call options with strike price $K e^{-(r-q)(T_2 - T_1)}$ and maturity T_1.

Problem 22.12.

Explain why a down-and-out put is worth zero when the barrier is greater than the strike price.

The option is in the money only when the asset price is less than the strike price. However, in these circumstances the barrier has been hit and the option has ceased to exist.

Problem 22.13.

Prove that an at-the-money forward start option on a non-dividend-paying stock that will start in three years and mature in five years is worth the same as a two-year at-the-money option starting today.

Suppose that c is the value of a two-year option starting today. Define S_0 as the stock price today and S_T as its value in three years. The Black–Scholes formula in Chapter 13 shows that the value of an at-the-money option is proportional to the stock price when there are no dividends. It follows that the value of the forward start option in three years is cS_T / S_0. We can now use risk-neutral valuation. The expected value of the option in three years in a risk-neutral world is $cS_0 e^{rT} / S_0 = c e^{rT}$. Discounting this to today at the risk-free rate gives c, proving the required result.

Problem 22.14.

Suppose that the strike price of an American call option on a non-dividend-paying stock grows at rate g. Show that if g is less than the risk-free rate, r, it is never optimal to exercise the call early.

The argument is similar to that given in Chapter 10 for a regular option on a non-dividend-paying stock. Consider a portfolio consisting of the option and cash equal to the present value of the terminal strike price. The initial cash position is

$$K e^{gT - rT}$$

By time τ ($0 \le \tau \le T$), the cash grows to

$$K e^{gT - rT} e^{r\tau} = K e^{g\tau} e^{-(r-g)(T-\tau)}$$

Since $r > g$, this is less than $K e^{g\tau}$ and therefore is less than the amount required to exercise the option. It follows that, if the option is exercised early, the terminal value of the portfolio is less than S_T. At time T the cash balance is $K e^{gT}$. This is exactly what is

151

required to exercise the option. If the early exercise decision is delayed until time T, the terminal value of the portfolio is therefore

$$\max[S_T, Ke^{gT}]$$

This is at least as great as S_T. It follows that early exercise cannot be optimal.

Problem 22.15.

Answer the following questions about compound options:

(a) What put–call parity relationship exists between the price of a European call on a call and a European put on a call?

(b) What put–call parity relationship exists between the price of a European call on a put and a European put on a put?

(a) The put–call relationship is

$$cc + K_1 e^{-rT_1} = pc + c$$

where cc is the price of the call on the call, pc is the price of the put on the call, c is the price today of the call into which the options can be exercised at time T_1, and K_1 is the exercise price for cc and pc. The proof is similar to that for the usual put–call parity relationship in Chapter 10. Both sides of the equation represent the values of portfolios that will be worth $\max(c, K_1)$ at time T_1.

(b) The put–call relationship is

$$cp + K_1 e^{-rT_1} = pp + p$$

where cp is the price of the call on the put, pp is the price of the put on the put, p is the price today of the put into which the options can be exercised at time T_1, and K_1 is the exercise price for cp and pp. The proof is similar to that in Chapter 10 for the usual put–call parity relationship. Both sides of the equation represent the values of portfolios that will be worth $\max(p, K_1)$ at time T_1.

Problem 22.16.

Does a floating lookback call become more valuable or less valuable as we increase the frequency with which we observe the asset price in calculating the minimum?

As we increase the frequency we observe a more extreme minimum. This increases the value of a lookback call.

Problem 22.17.

Does a down-and-out call become more valuable or less valuable as we increase the frequency with which we observe the asset price in determining whether the barrier has been crossed? What is the answer to the same question for a down-and-in call?

As we increase the frequency with which the asset price is observed, the asset price becomes more likely to hit the barrier and the value of a down-and-out call decreases. For a similar reason the value of a down-and-in call increases.

Problem 22.18.

Explain why a regular European call option is the sum of a down-and-out European call and a down-and-in European call.

If the barrier is reached the down-and-out option is worth nothing while the down-and-in option has the same value as a regular option. If the barrier is not reached the down-and-in option is worth nothing while the down-and-out option has the same value as a regular option. This is why a down-and-out call option plus a down-and-in call option is worth the same as a regular option.

Problem 22.19.

What is the value of a derivative that pays off $100 in six months if the S&P 500 index is greater than 1,000 and zero otherwise. Assume that the current level of the index is 960, the risk-free rate is 8% per annum, the dividend yield on the index is 3% per annum, and the volatility of the index is 20%.

This is a cash-or-nothing call. The value is $100N(d_2)e^{-0.08 \times 0.5}$ where

$$d_2 = \frac{\ln(960/1000) + (0.08 - 0.03 - 0.2^2/2) \times 0.5}{0.2 \times \sqrt{0.5}} = -0.1826$$

Because $N(d_2) = 0.4276$ the value of the derivative is $41.08.

Problem 22.20.

Estimate the interest rate paid by P&G on the 5/30 swap in Business Snapshot 22.4 if a) the CP rate is 6.5% and the Treasury yield curve is flat at 6% and b) the CP rate is 7.5% and the Treasury yield curve is flat at 7%.

When the CP rate is 6.5% and Treasury rates are 6% with semiannual compounding, the CMT% is 6% and an Excel spreadsheet can be used to show that the price of a 30-year bond with a 6.25% coupon is about 103.46. The spread is zero and the rate paid by P&G is 5.75%. When the CP rate is 7.5% and Treasury rates are 7% with semiannual compounding, the CMT% is 7% and the price of a 30-year bond with a 6.25% coupon is about 90.65. The spread is therefore

$$\max[0, (98.5 \times 7/5.78 - 90.65)/100]$$

or 28.64%. The rate paid by P&G is 35.39%.

CHAPTER 23
Credit Derivatives

Credit derivatives are contracts where the payoff depends on the creditworthiness of companies or countries. Usually the payoff is triggered by a default on outstanding debt obligations.

The most popular credit derivative is a credit default swap (CDS). This is designed to provide bond holders with insurance against defaults by a particular company or country for a period of time. The company or country is known as the reference entity. A notional principal is specified. The buyer of a CDS makes regular payments to the seller of the CDS. The payments are a certain percentage of the notional principal each year. This percentage is referred to as the CDS spread. (Thus if the CDS spread is 200 basis points the payments are 2% of the notional principal each year.) If there is no default, the buyer of the CDS gets nothing in return for the payments. If there is a default, the buyer has the right to sell bonds issued by the reference entity for their face value. The total face value of the bonds that can be sold equals the notional principal. You should study Tables 23.2 to 23.5 carefully to make sure you understand all the details of how CDSs work and how they are valued.

Note that the valuation of a credit default swap really involves nothing more than present value arithmetic. We calculate the present value of the expected payments and the present value of the expected payoffs. The CDS spread quoted for a new deal is the CDS spread per annum that equates the present value of expected payments to the present value of expected payoffs. Note also how the recovery rate is defined. It is estimated as the ratio of the value of a bond just after a default to the face value of the bond. It follows that the payoff from a CDS in the event of a default is $L(1 - R)$ where L is the principal and R is the recovery rate. Sometimes the payoff is made in cash rather than by the delivery of a bond. A calculation agent is then used to observe bond prices immediately after a default and estimate R.

The valuation of a credit default swap requires estimates of the risk neutral probabilities of default during each year of its life. These are sometimes estimated from bond prices and sometimes implied from the spreads quoted for credit default swaps themselves. (Estimating spreads from actively traded CDSs and using them to price other CDSs is analogous to what traders do when estimating volatilities for valuing options.) Make sure you understand the difference between conditional probabilities of default and unconditional probabilities of default.

Other credit derivatives you should understand are binary credit default swaps, basket credit default swaps, total return swaps, credit default swap forwards, credit default swap options, and collateralized debt obligations. Binary credit default swaps provide a predetermined cash payoff in the event of a default. Basket credit default swaps provide a payoff at the time of the nth default from a set of N companies ($N \geq n$). Total return swaps are agreements to exchange the total return on an asset (or portfolio of assets) for

154

LIBOR plus a spread. A credit default swap forward is an obligation to buy or sell a credit default swap in the future. A credit default swap option is the right to buy or sell a credit default swap in the future. Collateralized debt obligations are arrangements whereby the default risk on a portfolio of bonds is shared between different investors. Typically some investors have very little default risk exposure while others have high exposures.

SOLUTIONS TO PRACTICE QUESTIONS

Problem 23.8.

Suppose that the risk-free zero curve is flat at 7% per annum with continuous compounding and that defaults can occur half way through each year in a new five-year credit default swap. Suppose that the recovery rate is 30% and the default probabilities each year conditional on no earlier default is 3% Estimate the credit default swap spread? Assume payments are made annually.

The table corresponding to Tables 23.2, giving unconditional default probabilities, is

Time (years)	Default Probability	Survival Probability
1	0.0300	0.9700
2	0.0291	0.9409
3	0.0282	0.9127
4	0.0274	0.8853
5	0.0266	0.8587

The table corresponding to Table 23.3, giving the present value of the expected regular payments (payment rate is s per year), is

Time (years)	Probability of Survival	Expected Payment	Discount Factor	PV of Expected Payment
1	0.9700	$0.9700s$	0.9324	$0.9044s$
2	0.9409	$0.9409s$	0.8694	$0.8180s$
3	0.9127	$0.9127s$	0.8106	$0.7398s$
4	0.8853	$0.8853s$	0.7558	$0.6691s$
5	0.8587	$0.8587s$	0.7047	$0.6051s$
Total				$3.7364s$

The table corresponding to Table 23.4, giving the present value of the expected payoffs (notional principal =$1), is

155

Time (years)	Probability of Default	Recovery Rate	Expected Payoff	Discount Factor	PV of Expected Payoff
0.5	0.0300	0.3	0.0210	0.9656	0.0203
1.5	0.0291	0.3	0.0204	0.9003	0.0183
2.5	0.0282	0.3	0.0198	0.8395	0.0166
3.5	0.0274	0.3	0.0192	0.7827	0.0150
4.5	0.0266	0.3	0.0186	0.7298	0.0136
Total					0.0838

The table corresponding to Table 23.5, giving the present value of accrual payments, is

Time (years)	Probability of Default	Expected Accrual Payment	Discount Factor	PV of Expected Accrual Payment
0.5	0.0300	0.0150s	0.9656	0.0145s
1.5	0.0291	0.0146s	0.9003	0.0131s
2.5	0.0282	0.0141s	0.8395	0.0118s
3.5	0.0274	0.0137s	0.7827	0.0107s
4.5	0.0266	0.0133s	0.7298	0.0097s
Total				0.0598s

The credit default swap spread s is given by:

$$3.7364s + 0.0598s = 0.0838$$

It is 0.0221 or 221 basis points.

Problem 23.9.

What is the value of the swap in Problem 23.8 per dollar of notional principal to the protection buyer if the credit default swap spread is 150 basis points?

If the credit default swap spread is 150 basis points, the value of the swap to the buyer of protection is:

$$0.0838 - (3.7364 + 0.0598) \times 0.0150 = 0.0269$$

per dollar of notional principal.

Problem 23.10.

What is the credit default swap spread in Problem 23.8 if it is a binary CDS?

If the swap is a binary CDS, the present value of expected payoffs is calculated as follows

Time (years)	Probability of Default	Expected Payoff	Discount Factor	PV of Expected Payoff
0.5	0.0300	0.0300	0.9656	0.0290
1.5	0.0291	0.0291	0.9003	0.0262
2.5	0.0282	0.0282	0.8395	0.0237
3.5	0.0274	0.0274	0.7827	0.0214
4.5	0.0266	0.0266	0.7298	0.0194
Total				0.1197

The credit default swap spread s is given by:

$$3.7364s + 0.0598s = 0.1197$$

It is 0.0315 or 315 basis points.

Problem 23.11.

How does a five-year nth-to-default credit default swap work. Consider a basket of 100 reference entities where each reference entity has a probability of defaulting in each year of 1%. As the default correlation between the reference entities increases what would you expect to happen to the value of the swap when a) $n = 1$ and b) $n = 25$. Explain your answer.

A five-year nth to default credit default swap works in the same way as a regular credit default swap except that there is a basket of companies. The payoff occurs when the nth default from the companies in the basket occurs. After the nth default has occurred the swap ceases to exist. When $n = 1$ (so that the swap is a "first to default") an increase in the default correlation lowers the value of the swap. When the default correlation is zero there are 100 independent events that can lead to a payoff. As the correlation increases the probability of a payoff decreases. In the limit when the correlation is perfect there is in effect only one company and therefore only one event that can lead to a payoff.

When $n = 25$ (so that the swap is a 25th to default) an increase in the default correlation increases the value of the swap. When the default correlation is zero there is virtually no chance that there will be 25 defaults and the value of the swap is very close to zero. As the correlation increases the probability of multiple defaults increases. In the limit when the correlation is perfect there is in effect only one company and the value of a 25th-to-default credit default swap is the same as the value of a first-to-default swap.

Problem 23.12.

How is the recovery rate of a bond usually defined? What is the formula relating the payoff on a CDS to the notional principal and the recovery rate?

The recovery rate of a bond is usually defined as the value of the bond a few days after a default occurs as a percentage of the bond's face value. The payoff on a CDS is $L(1 - R)$ where L is the notional principal and R is the recovery rate.

Problem 23.13.

Show that the spread for a new plain vanilla CDS should be $1 - R$ times the spread for a similar new binary CDS where R is the recovery rate.

The payoff from a plain vanilla CDS is $1 - R$ times the payoff from a binary CDS with the same principal. The payoff always occurs at the same time on the two instruments. It follows that the regular payments on a new plain vanilla CDS must be $1 - R$ times the payments on a new binary CDS. Otherwise there would be an arbitrage opportunity.

Problem 23.14.

Verify that if the CDS spread for the example in Tables 23.2 to 23.5 is 100 basis points and the probability of default in a year (conditional on no earlier default) must be 1.61%. How does the probability of default change when the recovery rate is 20% instead of 40%. Verify that your answer is consistent with the implied probability of default being approximately proportional to $1/(1 - R)$ where R is the recovery rate.

The 1.61% implied default probability can be calculated by setting up a worksheet in Excel and using Solver. To verify that 1.61% is correct we note that, with a conditional default probability of 1.61%, the unconditional probabilities are:

Time (years)	Default Probability	Survival Probability
1	0.0161	0.9839
2	0.0158	0.9681
3	0.0156	0.9525
4	0.0153	0.9371
5	0.0151	0.9221

The present value of the regular payments becomes $4.1170s$, the present value of the expected payoffs becomes 0.0415, and the present value of the expected accrual payments becomes $0.0346s$. When $s = 0.01$ the present value of the expected payments equals the present value of the expected payoffs.

When the recovery rate is 20% the implied default probability (calculated using Solver) is 1.21% per year. Note that 1.21/1.61 is approximately equal to $(1-0.4)/(1-0.2)$ showing that the implied default probability is approximately proportional to $1/(1 - R)$.

In passing we note that if the CDS spread is used to imply an unconditional default probability (assumed to be the same each year) then this implied unconditional default probability is exactly proportional to $1/(1 - R)$. When we use the CDS spread to imply a conditional default probability (assumed to be the same each year) it is only approximately proportional to $1/(1 - R)$.

Problem 23.15.

A company enters into a total return swap where it receives the return on a corporate bond paying a coupon of 5% and pays LIBOR. Explain the difference between this and a regular swap where 5% is exchanged for LIBOR.

In the case of a total return swap a company receives (pays) the increase (decrease) in the value of the bond. In a regular swap this does not happen.

Problem 23.16.

Explain how forward contracts and options on credit default swaps are structured.

When a company enters into a long (short) forward contract it is obligated to buy (sell) the protection given by a specified credit default swap with a specified spread at a specified future time. When a company buys a call (put) option contract it has the option to buy (sell) the protection given by a specified credit default swap with a specified spread at a specified future time. Both contracts are normally structured so that they cease to exist if a default occurs during the life of the contract.

Problem 23.17.

"The position of a buyer of a credit default swap is similar to the position of someone who is long a risk-free bond and short a corporate bond." Explain this statement.

A credit default swap insures a corporate bond issued by the reference entity against default. Its approximate effect is to convert the corporate bond into a risk-free bond. The buyer of a credit default swap has therefore chosen to exchange a corporate bond for a risk-free bond. This means that the buyer is long a risk-free bond and short a similar corporate bond.

Problem 23.18.

Why is there a potential asymmetric information problem in credit default swaps?

Payoffs from credit default swaps depend on whether a particular company defaults. Arguably some market participants have more information about this that other market participants. (See Business Snapshot 23.3.)

Problem 23.19.

Does valuing a CDS using actuarial default probabilities rather than risk-neutral default probabilities overstate or understate its value? Explain your answer.

Real world default probabilities are less than risk-neutral default probabilities. It follows that the use of real world default probabilities will tend to understate the value of a CDS.

CHAPTER 24
Weather, Energy, and Insurance Derivatives

This chapter describes some non-traditional derivatives products. It considers how weather, energy, and insurance derivatives are typically structured.

The most common weather derivatives have payoffs dependent on the temperature at a particular weather station during a particular month. The temperature variable for a month is typically calculated as the cumulative cooling degree days (CDD) or cumulative heating degree days (HDD). The CDD for a day is $\max(A - 65, 0)$ where A is the average of the highest and lowest temperature in degrees Fahrenheit during the day. The HDD for a day is $\max(65 - A, 0)$. Popular contracts are forwards and options on the cumulative CDD or HDD during a month.

The three most important types of energy derivatives are oil derivatives, gas derivatives, and electricity derivatives. The oil derivatives market is a well established market where a variety of different contracts (such as futures, forwards, swaps, and options) trade actively in both exchanges and over-the-counter markets. Contracts typically relate to the delivery of a certain number of gallons of a certain type of oil at a certain location. The gas derivatives market typically involves forward contracts or options for the delivery of gas at a certain rate to a certain hub for the whole of a month. The electricity derivatives contract also typically involves forward contracts or options for the delivery of electricity at a certain rate to a specific location for the whole of a month. However, in the case of electricity the supplier may have the right the change the rate at which power is supplied during the month in certain ways.

Energy prices exhibit volatility and mean reversion. This means that prices fluctuate randomly, but tend to be pulled back to a long-run average level. Oil has a relatively low volatility and a relatively low rate mean reversion. For gas the volatility and mean reversion are somewhat higher. Electricity has a very high volatility and a very high rate of mean reversion. (This is largely because it is not possible to store electricity and so a day's demand must be met by electricity generation in that day.)

In a traditional reinsurance contract an insurance company pays other companies to take on risks it does not want to bear itself. An alternative to traditional reinsurance is a CAT bond. CAT bonds typically offer a higher rate of interest than regular bonds. However, the bond principal may be used to pay insurance claims.

SOLUTIONS TO PRACTICE QUESTIONS

Problem 24.8.

"HDD and CDD can be regarded as payoffs from options on temperature." Explain this statement.

HDD is $\max(65 - A, 0)$ where A is the average of the maximum and minimum temperature during the day. This is the payoff from a put option on A with a strike price of

160

65. CDD is $\max(A - 65, 0)$. This is the payoff from call option on A with a strike price of 65.

Problem 24.9.

Suppose that you have 50 years of temperature data at your disposal. Explain the analysis you would you carry out to calculate the forward cumulative CDD for next July.

It would be useful to calculate the cumulative CDD each July each year for the last 50 years. A linear regression relationship

$$\text{CDD} = a + bt + e$$

could then be estimated where a and b are constants, t is the time in years measured from the start of the 50 years, and e is the error. This relationship allows for linear trends in temperature through time. The expected CDD for next year (year 51) is then $a + 51b$. This could be used as an estimate of the forward CDD.

Problem 24.10.

Would you expect mean reversion to cause the volatility of the three-month forward price of an energy source to be greater than or less than the volatility of the spot price? Explain your answer.

The volatility of the three-month forward price will be less than the volatility of the spot price. This is because, when the spot price changes by a certain amount, mean reversion will cause the forward price will change by a lesser amount.

Problem 24.11.

Explain how a 5 × 8 option contract for May 2011 on electricity with daily exercise works. Explain how a 5 × 8 option contract for May 2011 on electricity with monthly exercise works. Which is worth more?

A 5×8 contract for May, 2011 is a contract to provide electricity for five days per week during the off-peak period (11pm to 7am). When daily exercise is specified, the holder of the option is able to choose each weekday whether he or she will buy electricity at the strike price at the agreed rate. When there is monthly exercise, he or she chooses once at the beginning of the month whether electricity is to be bought at the strike price at the agreed rate for the whole month. The option with daily exercise is worth more.

Problem 24.12.

Consider two bonds that have the same coupon, time to maturity and price. One is a B-rated corporate bond. The other is a CAT bond. An analysis based on historical data shows that the expected losses on the two bonds in each year of their life is the same. Which bond would you advise a portfolio manager to buy and why?

The CAT bond has very little systematic risk. Whether a particular type of catastrophe occurs is independent of the return on the market. The risks in the CAT bond are likely to be largely "diversified away" by the other investments in the portfolio. A B-rated bond does have systematic risk that cannot be diversified away. It is likely therefore that the CAT bond is a better addition to the portfolio.

CHAPTER 25
Derivatives Mishaps and What We Can Learn from Them

Derivatives markets have been responsible for some spectacular losses. It is important to understand what went wrong and how similar catastrophes can be avoided in the future. This is the focus of this final chapter.

The most important point to understand is that derivatives can be used in many different ways. They can be used to reduce the risks that arise from a company's operations or to take risks. It is important for all companies (financial and nonfinancial) to define clear and unambiguous risk limits and to set up internal controls to ensure that the limits are adhered to.

It is hard to believe that some of the events outlined in this chapter actually happened. It is important to recognize that the events are not representative of how derivatives are used most of the time. Most derivatives trades are entered into for sensible reasons. Overall the derivatives industry has been a huge multi-trillion dollar success story. It will be fascinating to see how it evolves in the years to come.